THE CONESTOGA WAGON

THE CONESTOGA SIX-HORSE BELL TEAMS OF EASTERN PENNSYLVANIA. Published by John Omwake for private distribution. Collaborators, H. C. Frey, H. K. Landis, Catherine P. Hargrave. Illustrated. 129 pp. Cincinnati: The Ebbert & Richardson Company.

THIS handsome quarto will be a joy to collectors and students of Americana. For its theme is one about which little has been written and sources of information are scanty, although the activity with which it deals was one of momentous importance and of a uniquely American character. Mr. Omwake was moved to the preparation of the book by his recollections of such teams in his boyhood, and he and his collaborators have searched far and wide and carefully in museums, historical societies, county histories, and what he calls "the hidden-away places of local history," for the voluminous and richly varied material he has brought together. There are chapters on the origin and name of the Conestoga wagon, the materials of which it was made and its construction, the horses that drew it, their harness and the bells with which they made music wherever they went, famous wagons and wagoners, the road to the West over which Conestogas traveled at the rate of 3,000 daily, the glories and incidents of wagoning when it was at its height, and other related matters. Mr. Omwake has, indeed, brought together all the facts and told the most nearly complete story about the Conestoga wagons and their six-horse bell teams possible at this time. He has made a contribution of much interest and value to the story of our early days. Not the least of the book's factors of interest are the copious and varied illustrations.

COPR. JOHN OMWAKE

Recollection of the Conestoga six-horse bell team of Wesley Koons, Franklin County, Pennsylvania.
Painted by E. R. Rollins for John Omwake.

THE
CONESTOGA SIX-HORSE BELL TEAMS
OF EASTERN PENNSYLVANIA

ও

PUBLISHED BY
JOHN OMWAKE
FOR PRIVATE DISTRIBUTION

CINCINNATI
THE EBBERT & RICHARDSON CO.
1930

COLLABORATORS

Mr. H. C. Frey,
    Historian,
    Harrisburg, Pa.

Mr. H. K. Landis,
    Landis Valley Museum,
    Lancaster, Pa.

Miss Catherine P. Hargrave,
    Cincinnati Museum Association,
    Cincinnati, Ohio

CONTENTS

LATE MR. WESLEY KOONS
of Franklin County, Pennsylvania
Whose Conestoga wagon and six-horse bell team
are still a happy memory.

SEARCHING into Museums, Historical Societies and the hidden-away places of local history in Eastern Pennsylvania, Maryland, Virginia, New York, New Jersey, New England, and even in England, has developed this little booklet.

I am deeply grateful to all these sources for their cordial helpfulness in gathering this data.

This book is dedicated to the memory of my Uncle Wesley Koons, and the recollections I have of his Conestoga six-horse bell team.

Wesley Koons operated a big farm near Greencastle, Franklin County, in Cumberland Valley, Pennsylvania. After the Civil War he was one of the few who kept up their Conestoga Bell Teams, to be brought to town on Election Day and on other public occasions.

These teams are a unique bit of Pennsylvania's early country life, and the small boy's ambition, to some day own and drive such a team, has led me to gather these bits of history into print.

JOHN OMWAKE.

PREFACE

ONE HUNDRED YEARS AGO wagoning was at its height, and on the Conestoga trail—the road from Philadelphia to Pittsburgh, which was the gateway to the Ohio country — were fleets of the great white-topped wagons. There were said to be three thousand daily, on this road alone. Some carried six or eight-ton loads of provisions and necessaries for the western country, and "back loaded" with furs and skins, flour and wheat, from the west for the eastern markets. Others carried families, who were going to the new country to make it their home, and all of their household goods.

Of contemporary records of all this activity there are few, and no stress is laid upon the wagons or their heavy six-horse bell teams. They were so much a part of every day that they are simply taken for granted.

Historians who wrote just after their era was past mention them only casually — they are still such a commonplace, as indigenous to the Pennsylvania countryside, as its farms and orchards, or its hills themselves.

References to the wagons are to be found in "An Old Turnpike Road," by Jacob L. Gossler; in "Wayside Inns," by Julius F. Sasche; "Old Pennsylvania Milestones," by Susan Carpenter Frazer; "Annals of Philadelphia," by John Watson; "The Old Pike," by T. B. Searight; "The Development of Transportation Systems in America," by J. L. Ringwalt; "History of Transportation in America," by Dunbar; and "Pennsylvania Province and State," by Albert S. Bolles. Most of the county histories of Pennsylvania make some mention of the wagon. Rupp's "History of Cumberland County" is the most lengthy account. In Scribner's Magazine for August, 1888, and in the National Geographic of November, 1923, there are articles about the Conestoga wagon and its horses. Alice Morse Earle has written entertainingly about the old wagon in "Home Life in Colonial Days" and "Stage Coach and Tavern Days."

Nevertheless, to most of us today, a Conestoga wagon means rather vaguely just any covered wagon. But it wasn't. The Conestoga wagon was a perfect vehicle for existing conditions and the highest type of a commodious freight carrier that has ever been known.

It started as a farm wagon and grew with the country. It rumbled farther and farther from its home farm — to the mill, to the market, and beneath its ponderous wheels trails widened and became roads, fords became ferries and then bridges, horizons broadened and the Conestoga wagon was the carrier between the east and the west, whose need George Washington had forseen.

Most of the material for this book has come from the Conestoga Valley in Lancaster County, where the wagons had their beginning. Mr. H. C. Frey has searched the countryside for the old wagons still to be found, and the reminiscences of their owners; while Mr. H. K. Landis, of the Landis Valley Museum, to whom the arts and industries of his county are an unfailing delight, has reconstructed from his treasures something of the spirit of the old Conestoga days, of the excellence of the craftsmanship and the sincerity of effort that went into their making.

Even standing silent in a dimly lit barn, the sturdy old wagon is splendid and impressive. With its six great sleek horses and the chiming bells it was the embodiment not only of the American tradition of strength and purpose, but of the joy of life. Perhaps Mr. Stevenson was thinking of it when he wrote "It is better to travel hopefully than to arrive, and the true success is to labor."

CHAPTER I

Of the Origin of the Conestoga Wagon and its Name

THE Conestoga six-horse bell teams of eastern Pennsylvania were as characteristic of the country as the great barns with stone ends, overhanging fronts, and elevated double-door rears; the old stone or brick houses and stone mills so often dated and bearing the names of their builders, and the worm and post and rail fences along the roads and around the broad fertile fields.

One of the milestones on The King's Highway, the Philadelphia-Lancaster road, built between 1733-1740.

They were rich rolling farmlands about the colonial metropolis of Philadelphia where, as early as 1698, two markets were held a week.* Chester, Germantown, Newcastle and Lewiston also had markets, that consumed the surplus of the immediate rural neighborhood. Conditions were quite different in New England, where everyone, even the doctor and the minister, farmed in a small way. There a span of horses was all that could be desired; but in Pennsylvania, where the farm wagon held twice as much as the wagon in New England, from four to eight horses were used.

Macaulay says that in England during the reign of Charles II, on the best highways, heavy articles were conveyed from place to place by stage wagons. On by-roads, and generally throughout the country north of York and west of Exeter, goods were carried by long trains of pack horses. The roads were so poor that six horses were necessary to draw a coach through the mud and ruts. A hundred years later, at the time of the American Revolution, English roads were still so bad that the cotton bales of Manchester were taken to Liverpool or

---

*History of Philadelphia, Scharf and Westcott.

Bristol on pack horses. George Sturt*, whose business was founded during the reign of Queen Anne, describes the English wagons as "large and cumbersome vehicles, with hind wheels six feet high or more and very wide" (meaning the tires). The farm wagon was called a wain, and the wagoner, a wainman. Carts with two wheels were also used both on the farms and for hauling on the roads. These were drawn by oxen, and the English were still using the two shafts

A Conestoga six-horse bell team, showing a man standing on the lazy board. Stage coach drivers drove from the right, and English coaches and other vehicles passed to the left. The Conestoga driver, however, drove from the left, and it was he who originated the American rule of passing to the right.
This is the wagon and six-horse bell team belonging to Mr. Amos Gingrich, of Lancaster.

after we had developed the single pole for a pair of oxen. Both carts and wagons naturally found their way to America.

The probability is that the first Pennsylvania wagons were modified English covered wagons, suggested by those of the English settlers in Chester and Delaware Counties, the carters' or farm wagons of England, rather short and wide, dumpy — but strong and serviceable. It was not what our farmer wanted, but it had the makings of a good wagon, and our wagon makers kept on improving it, largely at the suggestion of the purchaser, until a ponderous four-wheeled vehicle rumbled behind half a dozen strong draught horses.

*The Wheelwright's Shop, George Sturt.

The excellence of the wagons made in the Conestoga Valley of Lancaster County caused the name to become famous throughout the country, and the wagons were known as Conestogas. They were designed and built by local wheelwrights out of swamp oak, white oak, hickory, locust, gum and poplar, from the neighboring woodlands, and were ironed by the village blacksmiths. All of the work was, of course, done by hand.*

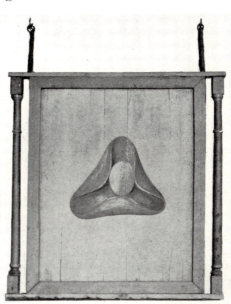

They differed from their English prototype in that the Conestoga wagon bed was long and deep and was given considerable sag in the middle, both lengthwise and crosswise, so that should the load shift, it would settle toward the center, and not press against the end gates; while the bed of the English wagon was flat and straight at the ends, and its bows, holding the white cover, were vertical. The bows of the American wagon, however, followed the line of the ends of the body, slanting outward and giving the distinctive and unmistakable silhouette of the Conestoga. Infinite variations occur, but always these characteristics remain.

The Sign of The Hat, a tavern in Leacock Township in Lancaster County, on The King's Highway. This sign was painted by Benjamin West and belongs to Miss Dorothy Flinn, Bleak House, Kinzers, Pennsylvania.

An early wagon bed, which is still to be seen in the Conestoga Valley, is graceful and boat shaped, and looking at it, it is easy to see why this wagon should have been called the Ship of Inland Commerce, as it cruised with its great white top between the green Pennsylvania hills.

Even had it not been for its striking contour, the Conestoga wagon would have been imposing because of its sheer bulk. The top of the front hoop was eleven feet from the ground. The white homespun cover was two dozen feet long. The top ends of the wagon bed were

*Doctor Mercer, of the Bucks County Historical Society, has written entertainingly about the tools that were made and used by the artisans of early Pennsylvania. See his "Ancient Carpenters' Tool" in Old Time New England. Boston, 1925-1928.

sixteen feet apart and the rear wheels five or six feet high. When the six-horse team was pulling, the team and wagon stretched to sixty feet.

The driver, instead of having a seat inside, rode on the lazy board, a sliding board of strong white oak that was pulled out on the left-hand side of the wagon body, when he was not walking beside his team or astride his saddle horse. From the lazy board he could operate the brake and call to his horses. The saddle horse was the wheel horse on the left-hand side. The wagoner was the first driver to drive from the left side. Coaches and all other vehicles of his day were driven from the right side; but the wagoner, for whom all other traffic had to make room, sat on the left and inaugurated the American custom of passing approaching traffic to the right instead of following the English rule of driving to the left.

The horses were as distinctive as the wagons. Early settlers in Pennsylvania had used small riding horses, sure footed, with great endurance, that could go any place. With the clearing of the land and the making of roads and interior settlements, it became necessary to develop a large type of horse capable of farm work and of hauling heavy loads long distances. In the early days of Lancaster County, grain had to be taken to the Downing Town or Brandywine mills, forty miles away, to be ground into flour.

William Penn is said to have had upon his estate at Pennsbury, three Flemish stallions of the draught-horse type, which were sent into the Conestoga Valley and bred with Virginia mares. Whether or not this is true, the characteristics of the Belgian draught horses persisted in the Conestoga breed, who had short arched necks, full manes, good legs and weighed fourteen hundred pounds and more.

Another possibility is that they were bred away from the English draught horses belonging to Penn's countrymen who had settled at Philadelphia and Chester, just as the coach or stage horse was bred away from the English race horse. At all events, in the leafy Conestoga Valley of Lancaster County, there was bred a race of large, patient, burden-bearing animals with sleek round bodies. They were well fed and never overworked, and so they arrived at a degree of perfection far surpassing the original stock. There seems to have been no scientific method of breeding. The colts were bridle broken at two and a half years, but seldom worked until they were three years old. Under kind treatment they throve. They were heavy, well set, of wonderful endurance — great horses for great wagons. Both bore the Conestoga name, which they were to make known throughout the land before their day was past.

A three-year old black Conestoga horse, owned by John Eshelman, Martic, Lancaster County. Height, 16 hands, weight 1,350 pounds. From the report of the Commissioner of Agriculture, Washington, D. C., 1863.

Their fame soon reached the dignity of tavern sign publicity. At Philadelphia, in the Pennsylvania Gazette of February 26, 1750, there is an advertisement:

"Just imported and to be sold very cheap for ready money by Thomas White, at his house in Market Street, almost opposite the sign of the Conestoga Waggon. Ben Weston's snuff, glassware, playing cards, etc."

Twenty-five years later George Washington wrote in his diary, under the date of May 17, 1775:

"Went to the commencement at the College, and din'd at Mr. Sam'l Griffin's. After wch. attended a Comee at the Conistoga Waggon."

This was undoubtedly the same old inn on Market Street above Fourth, and was kept by a Major Samuel Nicholls, or Nicholas. This committee was appointed to report to Congress a plan for the best means of protecting the province of New York by fortifications, troop stations, etc.*

Conestoga Creek in Lancaster County was named for the Indians, "the people of the forked roof poles" who lived along its banks. They had been an important tribe of Iroquoian stock in the country on the lower Susquehanna and about the head of Chesapeake Bay. The French called them Andastes, and the Virginians and southern colonists Susquehannas. They lived in palisaded villages and were brave and powerful. About 1675 they were overcome by invading Iroquois and some fled to North Carolina. The Iroquios took the rest captive to their own country. Later, they let them return, and like many other refugees, they found a home in Penn's Woods, and gave their name to one of its streams, where they lived happily and at peace with their neighbors.†

*The George Washington Diaries, edited by John C. Fitzpatrick.
†Dr. Thomas Lynch Montgomery, The Pennsylvania Historical Society.

CHAPTER II

Of some Wagons belonging to the Dutch Settlers at the Foot of a Mountain called the Blue Ridge

CONDITIONS were far from peaceful, however, on the northern and western frontiers in the middle of the eighteenth century. In 1745, in many issues of the Pennsylvania Gazette, Benjamin Franklin prints a proclamation of the Governor, Edward Trelawney, asking for volunteers against His Majesty's enemies, the "cruel and crafty French" and Indians.

During 1745 and 1746, his publication, "Quarter Waggoners," which he advertises with the Almanac, maps, books on remedies, etc., is really a pamphlet or broadside, urging the wagoners to enlist with their wagons and teams, in the king's service.

Ten years later General Braddock arrived in a glory of scarlet and gold, to defend His Majesty's domains against these marauders. Evidently the expedition was planned with the thought of George Washington's route of the year before in mind, for the English troops were landed at Hampton. In Virginia they were to acquire more men, provisions, and wagons for carrying these. Accordingly there were raised two companies of hatchet men or carpenters, six of rangers, and one troop of light horse.

*Captain Orme writes, "General Braddock apprehended the greatest difficulty in procuring waggons and horses, sufficient to attend him upon his march, as the Assembly had not passed an Act for supplying them, but Sir John St. Clair assured the General that the inconveniency would be easily removed, for in going to Fort Cumberland he had been informed of a great number of Dutch settlers, at a foot of the mountain called the Blue Ridge, who would undertake to carry by the hundred the provisions and stores, and that he believed he could provide otherwise two hundred waggons and fifteen hundred carrying horses to be at Fort Cumberland by the first of May." The wagons, however, were not forthcoming. It was the middle of April before the troops were all assembled at Will's Creek, where the

---

*The Journals of Robert Orme. February 20 — August 1, 1755. Edited by Winthrop Sargent.

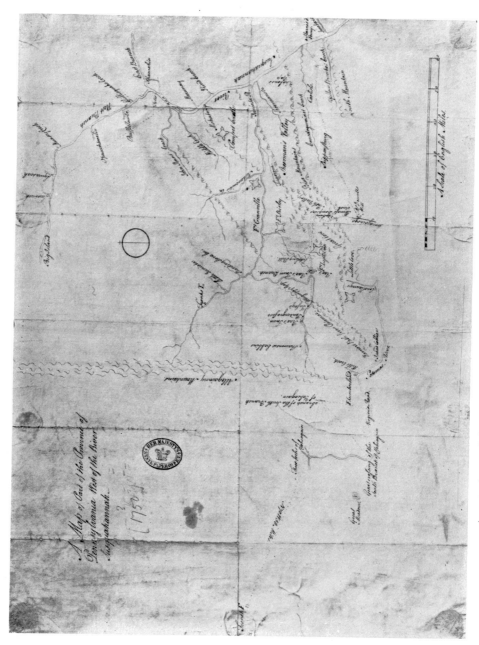

A map of part of the Province of Pennsylvania, west of the River Susquahannah.
From the original in the British Museum.

forest trail began, and even here there were insufficient supplies because of the inadequate transportation facilities.

It was at this point that General Braddock appealed for help to Benjamin Franklin, who describes the collection of the wagons in his autobiography. He says, "We found the General at Frederictown, waiting impatiently for the return of those he had sent through the back parts of Maryland and Virginia to collect waggons. * * * * When I was about to depart, the returns of the waggons to be obtained were brought in, by which it appeared they amounted only to twenty-five, and not all of those in serviceable condition. The General and all the officers were surprised, declared the expedition was then at an end, being impossible, and exclaiming against the ministers for ignorantly landing them in a country destitute of the means of conveying their stores, baggage, etc., not less than one hundred and fifty waggons being necessary. I happened to say that I thought it a pity they had not landed rather in Philadelphia, as in that country almost every farmer had his waggon. The General eagerly laid hold of my words and said, 'Then you, sir, who are a man of interest there, can probably procure them for us, and I beg you will undertake it.' I asked what terms were to be offer'd the owners of the waggons, and I was desired to put on paper the terms that appeared to me necessary. This I did, and they were agreed to and a commission and instructions accordingly prepared immediately. What those terms were will appear in the advertisement I publish'd as soon as I arrived at Lancaster, which, being from the great and sudden effect it produced a piece of some curiosity, I shall insert it at length.

"Whereas, 150 waggons with four horses to each waggon and 1,500 saddle or pack horses are wanted for the service of His Majesty's forces now about to rendezvous at Will's Creek, and His Excellency General Braddock having been pleased to contract for the hire of the same, I hereby give that I shall attend for that purpose at Lancaster from this day to next Wednesday evening, and at York from next Thursday morning to Friday evening, where I shall be ready to agree for waggons and teams or single horses on the following terms:

"1. That there shall be paid for each waggon with four good horses and a driver 15 shillings per diem, and for each able horse with a

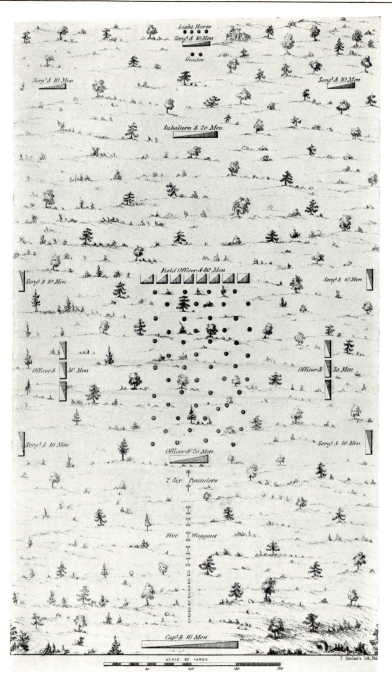

Plan of the distribution of General Braddock's advanced party,
showing the placing of the wagons.
From the Memoires of Captain Orme, edited by Winthrop Sargent.

pack saddle or other saddle and furniture, two shillings per diem, and for each able horse without a saddle 18 pence per diem.

"2. That the pay commence from the time of their joining the forces at Will's Creek and home again for their discharge.

"3. Each waggon and team and every saddle and pack horse is to be valued by indifferent persons chosen between me and the owner, and in the case of a loss of any waggon, team, or other horse in the service, the price according to such valuation is to be allowed and paid.

"4. Seven days' pay is to be advanced and paid in hand by me to the owner of each waggon and team or horse at the time of the contract if requested, and the remainder is to be paid by General Braddock or by the paymaster of the army at the time of the discharge, or from time to time, as it shall be demanded.

"5. No drivers of waggons or persons taking care of the hired horses are on any account to be called upon to do the duty of soldiers, or to be otherwise employed than in conducting or taking care of waggon horses.

"6. All oats, Indian corn or other forage that waggons or horses bring to the camp, more than is necessary for the subsistence of the horses, is to be taken for the use of the army and a reasonable price paid for same.

"Note — My son, William Franklin, is empowered to enter into like contracts with any person in Cumberland County."

Needless to say, the quota was completed and the Conestoga Wagon started on its first long trek into the west country.

An advertisement was also run in the Pennsylvania Gazette of May 22d, 1755, "Forty-one waggons are immediately needed, to carry each a Load of Oats and Indian Corn from Philadelphia to Will's Creek, for which they are to be paid at their Return Twelve Pounds each Waggon. Protections and Passes will be given the Waggoners by Authority of the General, to prevent their being impressed or detained after Delivery of their Loads. They are to set out together on Thursday the 29th Instant. Apply to Benjamin Franklin, in Philadelphia. Note — Several Neighbors may conveniently join in fitting out a Waggon, as was lately done in the Back Counties. If the Waggons cannot thus be obtained, there must be an impress."

With the moving forward of the expedition, the troubles centered on the wagons. George Washington wrote, "There has been vile management in regard to horses," and Captain Orme describes the situation in detail: "Most of the horses which brought up the train were either lost or carried home by their owners, the nature of the country making it impossible to avoid this fatal inconvenience, the whole being a continued forest for several hundred miles, without

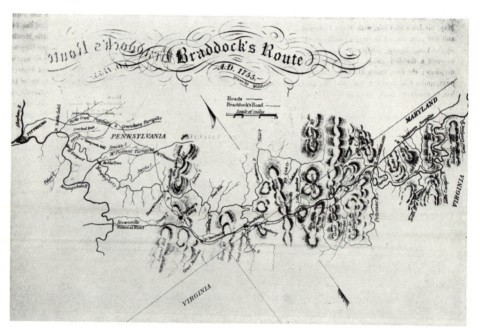

The National Road follows Braddock's Road from Will's Creek (Fort Cumberland), at the headwaters of the Potomac, to Fort Necessity at Laurel Hill. There Braddock's Road goes on almost due north while the National Road continues west. From the Memoires of Captain Orme, edited by Winthrop Sargent.

inclosures or bounds by which horses can be secured; they must be turned into the woods for their subsistence and feed upon leaves and young shoots of trees. Many projects, such as belts, hobbles, etc., were tried, but none of these were a security against the wildness of the country and the knavery of the people we were obliged to employ; by these means we lost our horses almost as fast as we could collect them, and those which remained grew very weak, so we found ourselves every day less able to undertake the extra-ordinary march we were to perform."

"The General, to obviate as much as possible these difficulties, appointed a Waggon Master General, and under him waggon masters over every forty waggons; and horse Masters over every hundred horses, and also a drover to every seven horses; the waggon and horse masters with the drovers were to go into the woods with their respective divisions, to muster their horses every night and morning, and to make a daily report to the Waggon Master General, who was to report to the General. * * General Braddock had applied to the Governor

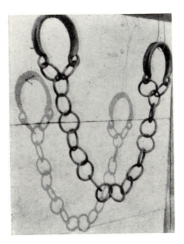

Horse hobbles to prevent team horses from straying far from open camps.
One of the end links has a bend in it, which passes under the hook of the collar and locks the hobble.
Landis Valley Museum.

of Pennsylvania soon after his arrival in America, to open a road from that country toward the Ohio, to fall into his road to that place from Fort Cumberland, either at the great meadows, or at the Yoxio Geni, that he might keep open a communication with Pennsylvania either for reinforcements or convoys. * * * * The Governor, through his Zeal for His Majesty's service, had it carried into great forwardness in a very short time. Mr. Peters, the Secretary of Pennsylvania, who had been to inspect the road, waited upon the General at Fort Cumberland to inform him of its progress; The General desired Mr. Peters would, in conjunction with Governor Morris, make a contract in his name for a magazine of provisions, to be formed at Shippensburgh, sufficient to subsist three thousand men for three months and to be completed by the first of July; * * * * * * * *   The General also fixed with Mr. Peters that the junction of the two roads should be at the Crow Foot of the Yoxio Geni.* The waggons, Artillery and carrying horses were formed into three divisions, and the provisions disposed of in such a manner as that each division was to be victualled from that part of the line it covered, and a commissary was appointed to each. The waggon masters were to attend their respective divisions to proportion the goodness of teams and to assist at every steep ascent by adding any number of horses from other waggons, till their respective divisions

*The union of the Youghiogheny, the Laurel Hill Creek and Castleman's River in Somerset County is commonly called the Turkey Foot or Crow Foot.

had passed. The waggoners were subdivided again into smaller divisions, every company having a certain number which they were to endeavor to keep together however the line might be broke. * * * * The form of the encampment differed very little from that of the march. Upon coming to the ground, the waggons were to draw up in close order in one line, the road not admitting more. * * * When the waggons were all closed up the waggon and horse masters were to assemble in some particular place their respective divisions and to give their orders to the waggoners and drovers. The horses were then to be turned out within the centinels, every centinel having orders not to suffer any horse to pass him.

"The detachment of six hundred men, commanded by Major Chapman, marched the thirtieth of May at daybreak, and it was night before the whole baggage had got over a mountain about two miles from the camp. The ascent and descent were almost a perpendicular rock; three waggons were entirely destroyed, which were replaced from the camp, and many were extremely shattered.

"June 11th. The General called a council of war * * * * in which it was agreed to send back two six-pounders, four cohorns, some powder and stores, which cleared near twenty waggons. All the King's waggons were also sent back to the fort, they being too heavy and requiring large horses for the shafts, which could not be procured; and country waggons were fitted for the powder in their stead. * * * The loads of all the waggons were to be reduced to fourteen hundred weight; seven of the most able horses were chosen for the howitzers, and five to each twelve pounder, and four to each waggon."

After ten days of struggling over the mountains, through the dark pine forest on a twelve-foot trail, they came to Little Meadows, twenty-four miles from Will's Creek. Here, to Washington's relief, General Braddock decided to "move forward with a detachment of the best men, and as little encumbrance as possible. * * * * * And on the nineteenth the General marched with a detachment of one Colonel, one Lieutenant Colonel, one Major, the two eldest Grenadier Companies and five hundred rank and file. The party of Seamen and eighteen light horse, and four howitzers with fifty rounds each, and four twelve-pounders with eighty rounds each, and one hundred rounds of ammunition for each man, and one waggon of Indian presents; the whole number of carriages being about thirty. The howitzers had each nine horses, the twelve-pounders seven, and the waggons six. There was also thirty-five days' provision carried on horses.

"Three hundred men with the miners (of whom the General had formed a company) had already been employed several days upon that hill.

"The General reconnoitered this mountain, and determined to set the engineers and three hundred more men at work upon it, as he thought it impassable by howitzers. He did not imagine any other road could be made, as a reconnoitering party had already been to explore the country; nevertheless, Mr. Spendlow, Lieutenant of the Seamen, a young man of great discernment and abilities, acquainted the General that in passing that mountain he had discovered a Valley which led quite round the foot of it. A party of an hundred men with an engineer was ordered to cut a road there, and an extreme good one was made in two days, which fell into the other road about a mile on the other side of the mountain."

Conditions were bettered, but there was still much to be desired. The soldiers complained of the severe and unusual labors, and even Washington succumbed to the effects of poor and insufficient food and arrived at General Braddock's camp on Thicketty Run on July sixth, ill, in a covered wagon.

In his account of the tragic ending of the expedition, Benjamin Franklin says, "the waggoners took each a horse out of his team and scamper'd." They all seem to have lived to fight another day. One of them, Daniel Morgan of Virginia, became a brigadier general in the Revolution. The wounded were taken back to Dunbar's camp at Laurel Hill in wagons, and there all the stores and ammunitions were destroyed and one hundred and fifty wagons burned.

Three years later the expedition under General John Forbes marched from Philadelphia with three hundred Royal Americans, twelve hundred Highlanders, sixteen hundred Virginians, twenty-seven hundred Pennsylvanians, and a thousand wagons, to take possession of the fort at the Forks of the Ohio. Most of these must have been the King's Wagons, as the provinces could hardly have supplied so many of their local ones. A line of forts had sprung up along the frontier since the Braddock defeat, and the road followed these. The

King's Highway led from Philadelphia to Lancaster. From there they marched to Harris' Ferry, where a stockade had been built in 1755; to Fort Lowther, eighteen miles southwest of Harrisburg, where Carlisle is today, over the road cut in 1755 at General Braddock's request to Shippensburgh, where Fort Morris had been built in the same year, to Fort Chambers, Fort Loudon, Fort Lyttleton to Fort Bedford. When the expedition arrived at the Forks of the Ohio it was to find the spot deserted, and Fort Duquesne, garrisoned by English troops, became Fort Pitt.

CHAPTER III

Of the Farm Wagon at Mount Vernon, and others used in the
Province of Pennsylvania

UNFORTUNATELY, few colonial farmers kept diaries or we might know considerably more about the Conestogas of the eighteenth century than we do. Washington makes constant mention of his farm wagon in his diaries and we can take it for granted that other landowners throughout Virginia and Pennsylvania were using theirs in the same way. On Sunday, January 20, 1760, he writes, "My Wagon, after leaving 2 Hogsheads of Tobo. at Alexandria, arrived here with 3 sides of sole Leather and 4 of upper Leather, 2 Kegs of Butter, one of which for Colo. Fairfax, and 15 Bushels of Salt, which She took in at Alexandria.

A most unusual old Conestoga wagon, having thirteen bows, belonging to Mr. M. K. Burgner of Chambersburg.

"Wednesday, 23rd. My Waggon set of for Frederick with Sundry's that were wrote for by the Overseer there.

"Thursday, February 7th. I went to Mr. Craig's Funeral Sermon at Alexandria and there met my waggons with 4 Hhds Tobo more. Unloaded and sent them down to Mount Vernon.

"Saturday, 9th. Set my Waggon's to draw in Stocks and Scantling, and wrote to Mr. Stuart of Norfolk for 20 or 30 more thous'd Shingles, 6 Barr'ls Tar, 6 of Turpentine and 100 wt of Tallow or Myrtle wax, or half as much candles.

"Monday, 18th. Dispatch'd my Waggon with Tools, etca., for Frederick. Sent over two more Tons of Hay — to Mr. Digges.

Rear view of the Burgner wagon, which is said to have been built in 1762 for a miller, Jonathan Keefer, of the Cumberland valley.

"Friday, 22nd. Upon my return found one of my best Waggon horses (namely Jolly) with his right foreleg mashd to pieces, which I suppose happend in the Storm last Night by Means of a Limb of a tree or something of that sort falling upon him. Did it up as well as I could this night.

"April, 1760 — Thursday, 10th. Val Crawford brought 4 Hhds of my Mountain Tobo. to the Warehouses in Alexa, two in my own Waggon, and with a Plow such as they use mostly in Frederick.

"July 26, 1767 — Waggon to be down.

"September 7, 1769 — Where & How my time is Spent. Dined alone. Vale Crawford's Waggon came up for my Goods in the Evening.

"April 28, 1770 — Remarks and Occurences. Cleveland's Waggon and Team began to work for me.

"May 9, 1770 — Remarks and Occurs. Discharged Cleveland's Waggon."

In October of this year Washington again went out to the Forks of the Ohio. In his own words on October 5th, "Began a journey to the Ohio in Company with Docr. Craik, his Servant and two of mine, with a lead Horse with Baggage." On the thirteenth, they "set out about Sunrise, breakfasted at the Great Meadows thirteen miles off, and reached Captn Crawford's about 5 O'clock * * * * * * Craw-

The Burgner wagon, showing the feed trough on the tongue. It is also equipped with the original locking chains, tar bucket and two tool boxes, one on each side. The old wagon, drawn by six horses, appeared a few months ago in a pageant given by The Penn Hall School for Girls of Chambersburg.

The Burgner wagon — The rear wheels are 5' 6" in diameter, and the front wheels 3' 10", and the tires are four inches wide. The hub caps are missing. The hubs measure nine inches at their small ends and twelve inches at their large ends.

The wagon bed is said to have been made at Waynesboro. It is four feet deep, fourteen feet long at the bottom and nineteen at the top. Its capacity is ten tons.

fords is very fine Land; lying at Yaughyaughgane, at a place commonly called Stewart's Crossing." On Sunday the fourteenth he writes, "At Captn. Crawford's all day. Went to see a Coal Mine not far from his house on the Banks of the River; the Coal seemed to be of the very best kind, burning freely and abundance of it." On the seventeenth they arrived at Fort Pitt "distant from the Crossing 43½ Measured Miles. * * * * * * We lodged in what is called the Town, distant about 300 yards from the Fort, at one Mr. Semples, who keeps a very good House of Publick Entertainment; these Houses, which are built of Logs and ranged into Streets, are on the Monongahela, and I suppose may be abt. 20 in Number and inhabited by Indian Traders, etca."

On the twentieth, they "Imbarked in a large Canoe" and for a month explored the wilds of the Ohio country. He writes of the wild geese which abound, of the ducks and innumerable quantities of wild turkeys, and of many deer watering and browsing on the wooded shore. Up the Kanawha, where the shore is grown up "with Hickory and oaks of different kinds, intermixed with walnut here and there," they shot buffalo.

On the journey back from Ft. Pitt to Virginia, on the twenty-sixth of November, is the entry "Reached Killiams on George's Creek, where we met several Families going over the Mountains to live, some without having any places provided. The

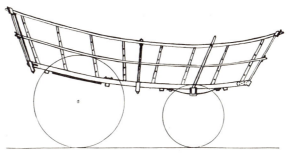

Illustrating curvature of bed and elevation of rear end of a Conestoga wagon in the Shreiner family of Landis Valley, Pennsylvania, since Revolutionary times. Length of bed at top is sixteen feet.

Codorus Forge on Codorus Creek, York County, built in 1765.

Snow upon the Alligany Mountains was near knee deep."

You wonder if these intrepid homeseekers were journeying with their household goods in white-topped Conestoga wagons.

On the first of December he arrived at Mount Vernon, after an absence of nine weeks and one day, a short time to have seen so much of the wilderness. On the eleventh he writes, "Agreed with Christr. Shade to drive my Waggon by the year, for the doing of which I am to find him in Bed, Board and Washing and to pay him eighteen pounds a year."

Roads were as invariably poor as the country side was rich, and the great sturdy wagons were kept busy, carrying the surplus from the farms into the towns and to the markets at Philadelphia and Baltimore. Much of the grain was converted into alcohol, or whiskey, the fruit into brandy or cider or vinegar, wheat into flour and flaxseed into linseed oil. Ten years after the revolution there were ninety-four grist mills and fifteen distilleries in Lancaster County alone, and all of the hauling was done by wagon.

Pottery was being made in Pennsylvania, and glassware and all of these things, as well as tobacco, were packed in barrels. These traveled safely in the boat-shaped wagons.

The iron industry was one of the earliest, requiring great strong wagons. Charcoal was the ironworker's fuel, and immense quantities were hauled from the forests to the furnaces, forges and bloomeries. It was a light load and a high wagon bed with outward flaring side boards was used. For the iron ore and pig iron, which was heavy, the bed was lower, with heavy floor planks placed crosswise, sometimes loose, so that the ore could be unloaded by prying up one plank after another and letting the ore fall beneath the wagon.

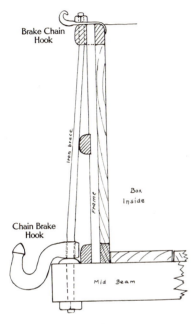

Sketch to scale of the side of an ore wagon from Safe Harbour at the mouth of the Conestoga. This hauled ore from the nearby magnetite and wash ore mine to the furnaces at Safe Harbour and probably to Martic Forge. It is a hilly country, the ore was heavy and the size of the load was limited to the pulling ability of the six horses, so this wagon bed is but 21" deep, but strongly made, using ⅞ or 1" boards inside instead of the usual ½ or ⅝". There was no cover and the rear wheels were higher than those of the road wagon and had 4" tires.

The first ironworks in Pennsylvania began operation about 1718, and ten years later four blast furnaces were working. Baron Stiegel built his furnace in 1757.

These wagons for heavy hauling were strongly made and well ironed. The running gear was about the same in all of them, the tires are said to have been six inches wide, the axles were protected by iron plates; the rear wheels were high, the hubs large and the axletrees heavy.

"An account of the European Settlements in America," published in London in 1761, the authorship of which is attributed to Edmund Burke, after alluding to the commercial enterprise of Philadelphia, says, "Beside the quantity of all kinds of produce of this province which is brought down the Rivers Delaware and Schuylkill, the Dutch employ between eight and nine thousand wagons, drawn each by four horses, in bringing the produce of their farms to this market."

A most unusual old wagon of this type belongs to Mr. M. K. Burgner of Chambersburg. It is said to have been built at Waynesboro, for Jonathan Keefer, a miller of the Cumberland Valley, in 1762. Its bigness is quite overwhelming. The wagon bed is fourteen feet long at the bottom and nineteen feet at the top and is four feet deep. It has carried ten tons of flour at a time.

The Shreiner wagon bed, stored at the end of the wagoning season. This was the usual method of storing. It is hoisted by a permanent windlass. The running gear is used for farm work. Note the curve of the body and the paneling. This is the forward end.

In contrast to this is the beautifully - proportioned old farm wagon belonging to the Shreiner family of Landis Valley. It was driven by Mr. Shreiner's great grandfather to Philadelphia, before the Revolutionary war.

Each year the wagon roads extended a little farther. In 1775 Richard Henderson and his party traveled into Kentucky with wagons as far as Captain Joseph Martin's station in Powell's Valley. From there they had to go with pack train.

THE VISION OF YOUTH AND THE FULL STRENGTH OF MANHOOD

A mural by Mr. J. Monroe Hewlett, in the Farmer's Trust Company of Lancaster, Pennsylvania, inspired by a speech of General LaFayette, which he made in 1825, on the site of the present bank. Courtesy of The Farmer's Trust Company, Lancaster, Pennsylvania.

CHAPTER IV

Of some Conestoga Wagons During the Revolutionary War and in the Years Following

ON THAT most momentous of days, July 4, 1776, Christian Noecker, farmer, of Dauphin County, arrived in Philadelphia with a wagon load of farm produce. Leaving his chickens and butter and eggs and other good things at the market, he joined the crowds who stood in the streets waiting to hear what Congress was doing — and when at last the Liberty Bell had rung and the declaration had been read publicly, "that these United Colonies are, and of right ought to be, free and independent states" there were cheers and the firing of guns, and when the darkness fell, bonfires and torchlight processions. In memory of these stirring events he bought a small and lovely Stiegel goblet with spiral stem, which is still treasured in his family.

During the hard winter at Valley Forge Conestoga wagons carried supplies to the American army. Mr. Nevin W. Moyer, of Linglestown, tells how his great, great, great, great-grandfather, Valentine Moyer, was master of the wagon train, and his son Philip one of the wagoners. It took much maneuvering to evade the redcoats, and it was only because they knew the country so well between Philadelphia and Valley Forge that they were able to get their supplies safely to the suffering army. Philip Moyer became an officer before the close of the war, and on his death his body was borne in his great Conestoga wagon to its final resting place, where the D. A. R., in 1923, placed a stone in his gallant memory. Valley Forge took its name from the forge of Isaac Potts, which had been there before 1770, and Washington was quartered at Mr. Pott's house. The farmers in the immediate vicinity had suffered great losses from the presence of both the American and the British armies and had grown indifferent as to the outcome of the fighting. They were loath to part with their small stores for worthless continental currency. *David Nelson was one staunch American who gave of all that he had. The shivering young

---

*David Nelson was the great-great-grandfather of Evelyn Omwake Bosworth.

soldiers cut fire wood on his wood lot and yoked themselves to sleds and hauled it to the camp. He opened his great barn doors and sent not only all of his grain, but the straw as well, to the sick and suffering boys who had not sufficient blankets. All winter supplies from the Nelson farm went to the hungry camp.

The Tavern Sign of The Three Crowns, painted by Benjamin West. The tavern it adorned was on The King's Highway, in Salisbury Township, Lancaster County. The holes in the sign were made by Continental bullets, so the Tory tavern keeper, to play safe, painted out the Three Crowns on one side of the sign and lettered it Waterloo Tavern. When the British were in the neighborhood The Three Crowns hung proudly beside his door, but when the Americans approached he turned the sign over, and it became the Waterloo Tavern. The original is in the collection of Miss Dorothy Flinn, Bleak House, Kinzers, Pennsylvania.

The next Spring, on April 16th, the Quartermaster advertises for "a number of experienced team drivers, to serve for one year from the time of enlistment, for which they shall receive ten pounds per month," and also "a number of good four-horse teams."

On December 20, 1778, "across the Conestoga Creek ¼ of an English mile wide, the water being very deep, the troops were taken to the other side in wagons." President Reed of the Second Provincial Congress wrote to General Washington in 1780, that "the army had been chiefly supplied with horses and wagons from this State (Pennsylvania) during the war," and that it was said that half the supplies furnished the army also came from there. Reed deplored the fact that a further demand for more than a thousand wagons was to be made, and said that the State could not stand it.

*In the Spring of 1778 a sturdy Conestoga wagon, drawn by four horses, and with a full company of Continental soldiers as a body-guard, brought six hundred thousand dollars in silver, the loan of the French Government, from Portsmouth, New Hampshire, where Louis' ship had landed, to the Government Treasury at York.

In the Fall of 1781 Washington twice mentions wagons in his diary. On August 21st he writes, "In the course of this day the whole of the American Troops, all their baggage, artillery and Stores, crossed the River (the Hudson); nothing remained of ours but some Waggons in the Commisarys."

"September 28th, 1781. Having debarked all the Troops and their Baggage, marched and encamped them in front of the city (Williamsburg, Va.), and having with some difficulty obtained horses and Waggons sufficient to move our field artillery, Intrenching Tools and such other articles as were indispensibly necessary, we commenced our March for the Investiture of the Enemy at York."

With the coming of peace, new problems confronted the new country, and because the Conestoga wagon solved some of these, it is interesting to read a few other entries in Washington's diaries.

"September 2, 1784. Having found it indispensibly necessary to visit my landed property West of the Appalachian Mountains * * * * * * I did on the first day of this month set out on my journey." (At Leesburg he bought a horse bell and a frying pan.)

"September 4th. Having finished my business with my Tenants (in Berkeley, Va.) and provided a Waggon for the transportation of my Baggage to the Warm springs, to give relief to my horses * * * * * * I set out after dinner. (The wagon was hired of W. Granthum, who was paid two pounds, two shillings for it, and his services for seven days.)

"Sep. 5th. Dispatched my waggon with the Baggage at daylight; and at 7 o'clock followed it.

"Sep. 6th. Remained at Bath (Warm Springs) all day and was showed the model of a Boat constructed by the ingenious Mr. Rumsey

---

*Brief History of York County. G. H. Prowell.

for ascending rapid currents by mechanism; the principles of this were not only shown and fully explained to me, but to my very great satisfaction exhibited in practice in private, under the injunction of Secrecy, until he saw the effect of an application he was about to make to the Assembly of this State for a reward. The Model and its operation upon the water, which had been made to run pretty swift,

A Conestoga wagon unloading bullion at the United States Treasury Building in 1778, now the First National Bank of York, Pennsylvania. From a painting in the Directors' Room, by courtesy of Horace Rudy.

not only of what I before thought next to, if not quite impracticable but that it might be turned to the greatest possible utility in inland Navigation and in rapid currents that are shallow — and what adds vastly to the value of the discovery is the simplicity of its works, as they may be made by a common boat builder or carpenter, and kept in order as easy as a plow or any common implement of husbandry on a farm."

(This was James Rumsey's first idea of the mechanical propulsion of boats; later he evolved the application of steam as the motive power, and shares with John Fitch the credit of being the inventor of the steamboat.)   All travel at this time was by water whenever possible, and the route to the west country was always from the head of one water course to the head of another.

The entry on the twelfth of September is, "In passing over the mountains I met numbers of Persons and Pack Horses going in with ginseng; and for salt and other articles at the Markets below."

Throughout this journey he comments on many occasions concerning various stretches of "Very good ground for a road."   On October 1, 1784, is the entry, "Dined at Mr. Gabriel Jones's."   (Mr. Jones was the leading lawyer of the Shenandoah Valley).   "His opinion is that the easiest and best communication between the eastern and western waters is from the north branch of the Potomack to Yohiogany or Cheat River; and ultimately that the trade between the two countries will settle in this channel.   In Ohio great Miame communicates with a river Sandusky, which empties into Lake Erie by short and easy portages; let us open a good communication with the settlements west of us — extend the Inland Navigation as far as it can be done with convenience.   No well-informed mind need be told that the flanks and rear of the United territory are possessed by other powers and formidable ones too, nor how necessary it is to apply the cement of interest to bind all parts of it together.   * * *   The way   * * *   is to open a wide door and make a smooth way for the produce of that Country to pass to our markets before the trade may get into another channel.   It is a long land transportation to Philadelphia for the people in the interior of Pennsylvania west of Laurel Hill — none is so convenient as the water way of the Yohiogany or the Cheat River to the Potomack."

In the succeeding years we get a picture of the wagon playing its important part on the farm.   "Thursday, March 10th, 1785.   Sent my Waggon with the Posts for the Oval in my Court Yard, to be turned by a Mr. Ellis at the Trng. Mill on Pohick, and to proceed from thence to Occoquan for the Scion of the Hemlock in my shrubberies.

"Friday, March 18th.   I went up to my Dogue Run Plantation to make choice of the size, and to direct the taking up of Pine trees for my two wildernesses.   Brought 3 Waggon Loads of them home, and planted every other hole round the Walks in them.

"Tuesday, November 15th, 1785. Went to my Neck Plantation and compleated the Acct of my Stock there except that of the Hogs, which stand thus: (There follows four pages of inventory, among the lists, Tools and Implements.)

"A Waggon Saddle and Gier for 4 horses.

"Two pr. Iron traces. N. B. These Traces serve the Waggon."

In 1786, Jack the waggoner is mentioned in a list of the negroes at Mount Vernon, which number 41 grown people and 67 children, and in September the wagon horses in their leisure are used for plowing at Dogue Run. The entry of November 13th of this year is, "Told James Bloxham, my farmer, who was about to write to England for his Wife and family, & who proposed the measure that he might write to one Caleb Hall a Neighbor of his in Gloucestershire (who had expressed a desire to come to this country and who he said was a compleat Wheelwright, Waggon builder & Plow & Hurdle maker) that I wd. give him 25 guineas a year for his Services (if he paid his own passage to this Country) the first year, & if I found he answered my purpose and we liked each other, that I might give him 30 guineas the next year & hold out encouragement if he chose to work for himself; that I would provide him with some place to live at whilst with me, that he should be found in Provisions, Washing and lodging.

A Conestoga wagon in the collection of the Ford Museum, Dearborn, Michigan. This is a good type with fine curve. The hub caps, bows and cover are missing. It came from Berks County.

"In the Spring of 1788 'the Waggon with two teams' is used for drawing scantlings to the New Barn, and fence rails, while throughout August and September the 'Waggon and the Ox Carts' were busy getting in the harvest of wheat, oats and rye at the various plantations."

Dr. Benjamin Rush, in his "Account of the manners of the German Inhabitants of Pennsylvania," which was published in Philadelphia in 1789, says, "A large and strong waggon, covered with a linen cloth, is an essential part of the furniture of a German farm. In this waggon, drawn by four or five large horses of a peculiar breed, they convey to market over the roughest roads between 2 or 3 thousand pounds weight of the produce of their farms. In the months of September and October it is no uncommon thing on the Lancaster and Reading Roads, to meet in one day from fifty to an hundred of these waggons on their way to Philadelphia, most of which belong to German farmers."

"They feed their horses and cows well, in such manner that the former perform twice the labor of those horses, and the latter yield twice the quantity of milk of those cows that are less plentifully fed. There is great economy in this practise, especially in a country where so much of the labor of a farmer is necessary to support his domestic animals. A German horse is known in every part of the state; indeed, the horse seems to feel, with his lord, the pleasure and pride of his extraordinary size."

A Conestoga wagon belonging to Colonel Henry W. Shoemaker, of McElhattan, Pennsylvania, made many trips to Baltimore and Pittsburgh, Harrisburg and Philadelphia. The wagon box was made about 1790, and was in the Books family for more than one hundred and twenty-five years. It is exceptionally well made and very ornamental. The front end gate is of rare construction, half of it being easily removable, so that the teamster could sit there to drive or a passenger ride there in state. In 1784 Pittsburgh is described as "a small place that does a great deal of small trade in wheat, flour, and skins, the goods being brought at the vast expense of 45 shillings per hundred weight from Philadelphia." The first wagons went out to Pittsburgh over the old military roads, which followed the pack horse trails, which in their time had originally been Indian trails. Between 1785 and 1790 the State cleared and widened the road from the Cumberland Valley to Pittsburgh.

These early wagons, known as Pitt teams, had bodies much more curved than those used on the farms or those that plied between Philadelphia and Baltimore. This was to keep the load from shifting as they went up and down the great ridges of the Alleghenies. Their tires were also narrower than those of the other wagons, because the roads were harder than those in the east.

CHAPTER V

Of The Conestoga Wagon Bells

DANIEL MOYER, son of Philip Moyer of Revolutionary fame, was born in 1766. From his home in Berks County he drove his team of great black horses to Philadelphia, Baltimore and finally to Pittsburgh, and more than one Black Horse Inn is said to have been named for them.

Whenever one wagoner helped another in distress on those rough or slippery roads, he received as a reward the hame bells of the hapless one, and Daniel Moyer and his fine team, a Saint Christopher of the new world, received many such tributes. These were usually little open bells suspended from flat iron hoops, the round ends of which pointed downwards and passed through eyes in the hames. The number and size varied, generally four to an arch, but sometimes three or five or even six; and each great horse plodded along to the leisurely lilt of the chime above his shoulders. Perhaps at first the bells were a necessity on the narrow wooded roads, just as horse bells were in the narrow English lanes, to warn other travelers of an approaching team. The Russians had a similar idea. A large bow was fastened upright from the shafts. They drove three horses abreast, the middle one in shafts. Generally there was a single bell at the top of the arch, sometimes more. Sleigh bells have been used in many countries. As to the Conestoga bells, Mr. Landis says, "We have them of welded iron, brazed iron, brazed bronze or brass, cast brass and turned brass, and, more recently, spun. Not one has a distinguishing mark to show where or by whom it was made, not even strings of sleigh bells. The motion of the horses wears the lug, whether passed through iron or leather, and the hole also wears, so that the bell as found today is generally fastened by a bolt or rivet. The pack horses that were used throughout the colonies always wore bells about their necks, which were kept from ringing in the day time but were loosened at night, so that the freed animals could be found in the morning. About 1785, in western Pennsylvania, pack horses were generally led in divisions

Hoop of bells, showing prongs to fit into the eyes on the wooden hames. Landis Valley Museum.

of twelve or fifteen, each carrying about two hundred pounds, all going single file and managed by two men, one going before as the leader, and the other at the tail, to see after the safety of the packs.* So invariable was the custom of the bell that a drover of pre-revolutionary days exclaimed, "Only think what a rascally figure I should cut in the streets of Baltimore without a bell on my horse!"†

Many a wagoner did not use bells on his saddle horse, because they interfered with his jerk line and whip and jangled beneath his very nose. For the wagoner rode a horse and not a wagon. The rear pair of horses were called the wheel horses, the one on the right being the off horse and the one on the left the saddle horse. The saddle was low but ample, after the English type, having a rounded pommel and brass-bound cantle with rings to fasten packages. The skirt was quite long and square cornered, while the stirrups were of brass or iron, although later they sometimes had wooden ones with leather guards. There was no useless ornamentation, but the leather was of the best. The team was guided by a jerk line to the forward, or lead horse.

Mr. Landis says, "We talked to a wagoner today (May 14, 1929) who used bells on his saddle horse. He said: 'They used three large bells on the wheel horse, four medium-sized ones on the second pair and five small ones on the lead horses.' I think that although wagon builders and outfitters stuck to a type, they had different ideas about many things. The more I learn

Another arrangement of Conestoga Wagon Bells.

*Watson's Annals of Philadelphia.
†Notes on the Settlements and the Indian Wars. Joseph Doddridge.

the more minor deviations I find, some of which don't belong at all, but that does not discredit the type; the exception but proves the rule. The old wagons flourished a long time ago and the trail has been rain washed and wind swept for so many generations that only here and there does the sign show. But every sign, however small, helps. For a long time, when we asked about team bells, we heard of nothing but bell-shaped brass. Now a man comes along saying he knows where there are six sets of bells entirely different. On each arch a big bell in the middle and two smaller ones on each side; but they are rectangular brass, with clappers outside, and they were slid over the

A Conestoga Six-Horse Bell Team, from Lancaster County, used by the Pennsylvania Railroad in a historical pageant of 1908. Courtesy of Mr. H. T. Wilkins, of the Pennsylvania Railroad, also of The National Geographic Society. Reproduced by special permission from "The National Geographic Magazine."

hame instead of through eyes in it. My mother says she remembers these square bells."

In a letter of August 9, 1929, Mr. William H. Breithaupt, of the Historical Society of Kitchener, Ontario, writes: "You asked me in a letter of April 25 about bells on teams drawing settlers' wagons. Curiously enough, we have just received what may be called a chime of bells, which came on the back of a horse, one of a four-horse team, driven by Samuel Bricker, who came to this locality from Pennsylvania in 1802.

"There are eight bells mounted on a broad double strap or thong, the bells spherical, varying from three inches in diameter to two inches, and giving a pleasing composite sound together. They are quite loud, and could, I think, have been heard a quarter of a mile away through the woods."

Only last week a Kentucky farm wagon and bell team drove into the sunset on a blue grass by-road, where the foothills of the Cumberlands commence.

"In colonial times there were bells of all kinds. Who made them? Bishop's American Manufacturer's lists makers of cast brass, likewise of large church bells, but none of small bells. They had bells on turkeys, on sheep, on cattle and horses; they had strings of bells for sleigh horses, big ones and little ones, rectangular and bell-shaped; I just heard an old lady say that she had seen Conestoga bells shaped like cow bells, but small and of brass. Dinner bells were common after 1800, and grazing bells were necessary before there were many fences. Any brass founder could make them. Some think they were made in New England. No doubt many were imported up to 1800. The Indians, less than a hundred years ago, made a bell fringe of tin, which tinkled when they struck each other. Where did they get the idea?"

In the Fourteenth Century bells were a favorite ornamentation of court attire, a badge of royalty, so that the German playing cards to this day have a suit of bells, typifying the nobility. While Saint Patrick and all the Irish saints who followed him had each his bell, which he "rang hardly" at a crisis, and by its mystic resonance the sick were healed, the Druids vanquished and the snakes put to flight. How far is it from a bell on the hill of Slane to those of the Conestoga trail?

CHAPTER VI

Of the Glory of Wagoning, and the Road to the West

THE glory of wagoning developed with the growth of good roads, not much before 1800, and the great Conestoga farm wagon became the public freight carrier of the country. Great numbers of

The Upper Ferry Bridge built over the Schuylkill in 1805, showing a five-horse Conestoga team; from the engraving by Jacob Plocher, after Thomas Birch. The bridge took six years to build and was finished in 1805. On March 18, 1817, the following advertisement appears in the Lancaster Journal:

To Waggoners—Reduction of Toll

The Tolls at the Upper Lancaster Schuylkill Bridge, are reduced to the following rates, viz.:

Six-horse waggon	*14½ cts.*	*Three-horse waggon*	*7½ cts.*
Five-horse waggon	*12½ cts.*	*Two-horse waggon*	*6¼ cts.*
Four-horse waggon	*10 cts.*	*One-horse waggon*	*3 cts.*

All pleasure carriages the same as heretofore.

At the first Turnpike Gate on the Lancaster Road, there is a reduction in the Toll of 10 cents for a four-horse waggon passing over the Upper or Lancaster Schuylkill Bridge, and a proportionate reduction in all other tolls, making a saving equal to the toll of the bridge.

the farm wagons still took their big loads to more or less distant markets and mills, but other wagons, known as "Regulars," made a business of freighting, and made regular trips from Baltimore to Philadelphia or from Philadelphia to Lancaster, and later over the western mountains to the new town of Pittsburgh.

The wagon itself was picturesque and impressive. Its wheels and removable side boards were painted a bright vermilion, while the running gear was a soft blue, and the high white cover gleamed in the sunshine, a brave sight, cruising between the green fields and the wooded hills. Many a wagon was driven by its owner or his son, and many drivers owned their own farms. A wagoner was selected because of his ability and dependability, and when anyone interfered with his charge he knew how to defend his rights.   He was a sturdy and stalwart American, and not only a local hero because of his courage and strength, but a doer of really great deeds and an empire builder.   Many are the tales of his prowess.   Daniel Moyer, in a contest of strength with a rival, went to Charming Forge, where a half ton of pig iron was placed on the back of each man.   Moyer walked away with his, while the other could not stir from the spot.

In 1789 Jacob Bowman, of Hagerstown, drove his Conestoga, drawn by four horses and carrying a load of two thousand pounds, over the mountains by the southern route to Brownsville, where he settled. There is great interest in this little known western country in the years immediately following the Revolution.   In 1790 Washington writes in his diary of trouble with "Vagabond Indians," which is promptly quenched by the "Regular Troops with their headquarters at Fort Washington (Cincinnati)."   The action took place in the Paint Creek valley, which he says is "the finest land in the world." Four years later, in October of 1794, he writes of breakfasting in Greencastle, in Franklin County, and follows with a description of the countryside about Reading, Lebanon, Harrisburgh, Carlisle and Shippensburgh, and the roads connecting them.   In the Pittsburgh Centinel of the same year, the Ohio packet boats are advertised, armed keel boats of twenty or thirty tons, which made the journey from Pittsburgh to Cincinnati in twelve days.   The advertisement says persuasively that the proprietors of these two boats have maturely considered the many inconveniences and dangers hitherto incidental to navigation upon the Ohio, and "influenced by a love of philanthropy and a desire of being serviceable to the public, have taken great pains to render the accommodations on board as agreeable and convenient as they could possibly be made.   No danger may be apprehended from the enemy, as every person on board will be under cover made proof to rifle balls, and convenient port holes for firing out."   Not all of the adventure was for the Conestoga wagoner.

In 1796 Francis Baily, an Englishman, traveled out to the Ohio country, and kept a diary.   Like most travelers they went on horseback, but their baggage followed by wagon.   He writes, "I have seen ten or twenty wagons at a time on their way to Pittsburgh and other

parts of the Ohio.   These are loaded with the clothes and necessaries
of a number of poor emigrants who follow on foot with their wives
and families, who are sometimes indulged with a ride when they are
tired or in bad weather.   In this manner they will travel and take
up their abode in the woods on the side of the road like gypsies in
our country."   His description of the majesty of the mountains and
the forests in the silver moonlight is worth reading.   He says, "The
roads, which are carried over the mountains, are much better than I

*A Conestoga wagon belonging to the Ford Historical Museum at Dearborn, showing all of the
equipment, and the feed box on the tongue.   Note the fine set of this wagon.   Mr. Landis says
"Some wagons seem low behind because, in putting on the bed, they did not first put the bolster
over the rear axle: it makes a great difference in the looks of the wagon.   A good rooster carries
his tail high, and not trailing behind."*

expected, and if from the tops of them you can, through an opening
of the trees, gain a view of the surrounding country, it appears a sea
of woods and all those hills, which appeared very high in our passing
over them, are lost in one wide plane extending as far as the eye can
see — at least fifty or sixty miles.   The wagons which come over the
Allegheny Mountains from the Atlantic states, bringing dry goods
and foreign manufactures for the use of the back country men, return
from this place (Pittsburgh) generally empty; though sometimes they
are laden with deer and bear skins and beaver furs, which are brought
in by hunters and sometimes by Indians, and exchanged at stores
for such articles as they may stand in need of."

In 1795 the Philadelphia-Lancaster turnpike was opened, and so
great was the travel on it that inns sprang up along its whole length.
In Chester County there was said to be one for every mile of road.

At night the yards would be filled with teams, the horses standing on each side of the wagon tongue, where the trough of feed had been placed, while the wagoner took his blankets and mattress, which he carried in a roll, and spread them on the floor of the hostelry, where he slept in company with many companions.

One of the oldest surviving wagons we know, of whose date we can be sure, is one at Kitchener, Ontario, belonging to the Historical Society. In 1807 Abraham Weber drove this from his old home in Lancaster county to his new one that he established in the Grand River Colony, and in 1812 other Conestogas, probably following the same trail, carried powder from the Dupont mills on the Brandywine to Commodore Perry at Lake Erie. After the war, some of them seem to have stayed in the north country, for great white-topped Conestogas, drawn by six or eight horses, became more and more numerous, carrying farm produce from the hills of Vermont and New Hampshire down to the seaports, Boston and Salem and Portsmouth, and bringing back products from the whole world. Their drivers were hearty, healthy Yankees, who besides being wagoners were traders, buying supplies for inland merchants, who seldom visited the cities.

Fortescue Cummings, writing "Sketches of a Tour to the Western Country," which was published in Pittsburgh in 1810, says, "On January 8, 1807, I left Philadelphia on foot, accompanying a wagon which carried my baggage. I preferred this mode of traveling for several reasons. Not being pressed for time I wished to see as much of the country as possible; the roads were in fine order and I had no incentive to make me desirous of reaching any point of my intended journey before my baggage. With respect to expense, there was little difference in my traveling in this manner, or on horseback, or in the stage, had I been unincumbered with baggage; for the delay on the road, awaiting the slow pace of a loaded wagon, which is not quite three miles an hour, and not exceeding twenty-six miles on a winter's day, will occasion as great expense to a traveler in a distance performed otherwise in less than half the time, including the charge of horse or stage hire.

"The first object which struck me on the road was the new bridge over the Schuylkill, which does honour to its inventor for its originality of architecture, and its excellence of mechanism. The bridge was six years in building, was finished in 1805, and cost in work and materials two hundred and thirty-five thousand dollars."

"There is a turnpike road of sixty-six miles from Philadelphia to Lancaster, which my wagoner left at Downingstown about half way, keeping to the right along a new road, which is also intended for a turnpike road to Harrisburg, and which passes through New Holland, where he had some goods to deliver. The face of the country between Philadelphia and Lancaster is hilly, and variegated with woods and cultivated farms. It is extremely well inhabited and consists of almost every variety of soil, from sandy and light to a rich black mould, which last quality is observable generally between New Holland and Lancaster, except on the heights on each bank of the Conestoga. The first settlers of all this tract were English, Irish, and German, but the latter have gradually purchased from the others, and have got the best lands generally into their possession.

Settlers wagon driven by Abraham Weber, who came to Kitchener, Ontario, from Lancaster County in 1807.
"The diameter of the front wheels is 37 inches, that of the rear wheels 49 inches, and the tires are 2¾ inches broad. The paneled wagon bed is 12 feet long, 3½ feet wide and 30 inches deep. The rear gate is in two parts, upper and lower. There are two cleats for hoops on every upright of the box paneling, eight in all. The wheels are held on the axle by linch pins, and the iron work is elaborate." W. H. Breithaupt, President of the Waterloo Historical Society.

"On Thursday, 29th of January, I left Lancaster on foot, proceeding along the Harrisburg Road, at a steady pace of about three miles and a half an hour. The weather was remarkably fine, and the road in excellent order, and what was remarkable for the season, a little dusty. About a mile and a half from Lancaster I passed a turnpike toll gate, from a little beyond which I got the last view of the steeples of that town, and soon after I crossed a branch of Conestoga Creek. The road continued fine, and the country rich, laid out in large farms, with good dwelling houses of brick and stone, and immense barns. Though hill and dale, woods, and cultivated farms presented themselves alternately, yet there was nothing very striking in the scenery. The road continued fine, nine miles, to a rivulet called Big Chickey, which crossed over an Indian bridge, which is a high tree cut down so as to fall across the stream from bank to bank, and then its branches lopped off. The banks being high, and the bridge long and narrow, my nerves were so discomposed when I reached the middle, that I had liked to have fallen off, but balancing and tottering, I at length reached the end.

"Two miles further I had to cross another Indian bridge over Little Chickey Creek, which I did boldly, without any difficulty, which is one proof of the use of practise and experience. The road now became very bad, the turnpike intended from Lancaster to Harrisburg not being as yet finished any further. The country also is not so highly improved as in the neighborhood of Lancaster, the inhabitants still residing in their original small log houses, though they have generally good and spacious stone barns. After four hours' walking I arrived at Elizabethtown, eighteen miles from Lancaster, and stopped at the sign of General Wayne, where for a five-penny bit (six cents and a quarter) I got a bowl of excellent egg punch, and a crust of bread.

"The road to Harrisburg leads parallel to the Susquehanna, in some places close to the river, and never more distant from it than a quarter of a mile, along a very pleasant level, bounded on the right by a ridge of low, but steep wooded hills, approaching and receding at intervals, and affording a fine shelter from the northerly winds, to the farms between them and the river; which is perhaps one reason that the orchards are so numerous and so fine in this tract.

"About three miles below Harrisburg the mountains terminate, and the south bank of the river becomes more varied, though still hilly; and here on an elevated promontory, with a commanding view of the river, from above Harrisburg to below Milleton, is a large and apparently fine stone house, owned by General Simpson, who resides in it on his farm, and is proprietor of a ferry much frequented by the western wagonners, as the road is shorter by two miles than that by Harrisburg. He farms out the ferry on his side for about three hundred dollars per annum, while on this side the proprietor rents it at four hundred and seventy. The value of this ferry, called Chamber's, may serve to convey some idea to the state of traveling in this country, particularly if one reflects that there are many other well-frequented ferries where public roads cross the river, within thirty miles both above and below this one, and which are all great avenues to the western country.

Conestoga wagons, taking powder from the Brandywine Mills to Lake Erie during the War of 1812, from a painting by Howard Pyle, made for the E. I. du Pont de Nemours Company. The wagon in the foreground was painted from the one belonging to Mr. Amos Gingrich, of Lancaster.

In 1913, in honor of the one hundredth anniversary of the Battle of Lake Erie, this sturdy old wagon once more made the long journey from the mills on the Brandywine to Lake Erie. Mr. S. W. Long, of the du Pont de Nemours Company, who had charge of the expedition, says that there seems to be no records in Washington of the Government's purchase of the powder. These may have been destroyed when the British entered the city and burned the White House in 1814, or the powder may have been sent as a gift, as the company's patriotism was well known. It is also an established fact that the powder used in the famous battle came from the Brandywine Mills in Conestoga Wagons.

"When within a mile and a half of Harrisburg, the white cupola of its courthouse, and roofs of the houses of the town are seen peeping over the trees, and have a good effect. At one o'clock I entered the town to the left over Paxton Creek bridge.

"On Saturday, 24th, I arose early, but the ferryboat not being ready I partook of an excellent breakfast with my friendly host and his family, and at ten o'clock I embarked in a large flat, with the western mail and several passengers and horses. The flat was worked by nine stout men, with short setting poles shod and pointed with iron, to break the ice and stick in the bottom. Only one sat or pushed on the upper side, while eight sat on the lower side, to keep the boat from being forced by the current against the ice, while a tenth steered with a large oar behind. A channel for this purpose had been cut through the ice, and was kept open, as loaded wagons could cross the river in a flat with more safety than on the ice.

"Ten miles further brought me to Carlisle, at six o'clock in the evening; the whole road from Harrisburg being fine and level, the houses and farms good, and the face of the country pleasant. The view on the right is all the way terminated by the Blue Mountains — the longest northeastern branch of the Allegheny ridge, from six to ten miles distant.

"Before I retired to rest I walked to the tavern where the wagons generally stopped, and had the pleasure of finding that arrived, which carried my baggage, which I had not seen since I left Lancaster.

"On the 25th of January at 8 a. m. I left Carlisle, having previously taken an egg beat up in a glass of wine. There are two roads, one called the Mountrock Road, which goes from the north end to the town, and the other called the Walnut-bottom Road, which leads from the south end. They run parallel to each other about three miles apart. I took the latter, which is the stage road, as the wagon with my baggage was to go that way, though I was informed that the first led through a better country.

"At eleven o'clock I stopped and breakfasted at a large tavern on the right, seven miles from Carlisle; I got coffee, bread and butter, eggs and excellent honey in the comb, for which I was charged only nineteen cents. My landlord presented me one of the largest and finest apples I had ever seen.

"As I proceeded from thence, two very beautiful red foxes playfully crossed the road about a hundred yards before me; they then recrossed it, and seeing me, made up a hill to the right with incredible swiftness, leaping with ease a Virginia worm fence above six feet high. At half past four I arrived at Shippensburg. I stopped at Raume's, a German House about the middle of the town, and apparently the best tavern in it. I bathed my feet in cold water, and dressed the left one, which was much blistered and very painful. Soon after which my wagonner Jordon, with three others in his company arriving, we all sat down together, according to the custom of the country, to a plentifully and good supper; after which, the wagonners spread their mattresses and blankets around the stove in the bar room, and I retired to a good bed, but without an upper sheet.

Conestoga Wagon and six-horse bell team, owned by Amos Gingrich, of Lancaster, Pennsylvania. The wagon was bought from Mr. Addison Longnecker, of Ephrata, and the bells from Mr. Isaac Wenger, of Lancaster County. This shows the wagon starting on its long journey to Lake Erie.

"On the morning of the 27th of January I took leave of my friendly host Skinner. After riding four miles on a continued ridge of the Sidelinghill, we stopped at a log tavern. It was a large half-finished log house, with no apparent accommodation for any traveler who had not his own bed or blanket. It was surrounded on the outside by wagons and horses, and inside, the whole floor was so filled with people sleeping, wrapped in their blankets round a large fire, that there was no such thing as approaching it to get warm, until some of the travelers who had awoke at our entrance went out to feed their horses, after doing which they returned, drank whiskey under the name of bitters, and resumed their beds on the floor — singing, laughing, joking, romping, and apparently as happy as possible. So much for custom.

"About four miles from hence, we descended the western side of Siidelnghill Mountains, here called Rayshill, at the foot of which we forded the river Juniata.   After crossing the Juniata we pursued our road through a broken country, very hilly, with the river almost always in sight, sometimes on one hand and sometimes on the other, as its bends approached or receded from the road, and sometimes directly under us at the foot of terrific precipices, down one of which, about twenty years ago, a wagon was carried by the horses, falling three or four hundred feet perpendicularly — the wagonner and horses were killed and the wagon was dashed to pieces.

"The 31st of January at four in the morning I left Bedford in the stage with three gentlemen and a young girl as passengers.   It had snowed all night, and the ground was covered some inches deep, so we had to proceed slowly to break the road, crossing the West branch of the Juniata twice in the first three miles.   As day dawned the country appeared to be in general rather more settled and cultivated than on the eastern side of Bedford, but it was still very hilly, and woods was the prevailing feature.   At half past 10, we had reached the foot of the Allegheny ridge, where we breakfasted; and here I found one of the advantages of traveling in the stage, was to be charged a sixteenth of a dollar more per meal than if one traveled in any other way.

"We were now in Somerset County, and having changed stages, horses, and drivers, we ascended by a very easy road of one mile to the top of the highest ridge of land in the United States, to the eastward of which all the rivers flow to the eastward, to empty themselves into the Atlantic Ocean, while to the westward they flow westerly to unite with the Mississippi, which is their common aqueduct to the gulf of Mexico.

"The face of the country before us is changed for the better; not being broken as to the eastward, but fine extensive levels and slopes, well inhabited and cultivated; and the ridges of the hills, though long, not so steep, and finely clothed with heavy wood.   This was the general appearance of the country, until we arrived at Somerset, the capitol of the county, fourteen miles from the top of the Allegheny ridge.

"The 1st February at 4 a. m. I left Somerset in a sleigh, a good deal of snow having fallen the day before.   At 10 a. m. we changed horses and our sleigh for a stage wagon, two miles from M'Mullen's at

M'Ginnis's, perhaps the dirtiest tavern on the whole road.   We then continued ten miles over a broken hilly country, with rich valleys, crossing a high ridge called Chestnut hills, from whence the western country is spread out under the view, like an immense forest, appearing flat from the height we were at, though it is in fact, as we found it, very hilly.   We crossed the river Sewickly, a fine millstream, by a bridge, ten miles from M'Ginnis's, and eight miles further we arrived at Greensburg, the capitol of Westmoreland County, which we entered at the eastern foot of Laurel hill.   Greensburg is a compact, well-built, snug little town, of about a hundred houses, with a handsome courthouse, a Presbyterian meeting house, and a market house.

"On entering Habach's tavern I was no little surprised to see a fine coal fire, and I was informed that coal is the principal fuel of the country fifty or sixty miles around Pittsburgh.   It is laid down at the doors here for sixty cents a bushel.

"At five o'clock next morning we resumed our journey, and found very little snow on the road, though there was so much on the mountains behind us.   The aspect of the country is similar to what it is between the Laurel hills and Greensburg.   Hills running in ridges from north to south, heavily wooded with white oak, walnut, sugar tree and other timber natural to the climate; and the valleys narrow, but rich and all settled.   At eight miles from Greensburg we passed on our right an excellent house and fine farm of a Colonel Irwin, one of the assistant judges; and three miles farther we stopped to change horses and breakfast at Stewart's, where we were charged only a quarter of a dollar each.

"We soon after entered Allegheny County.   At nine miles from Stewart's we descended a very long and steep hill by a shocking road, crossed Turtle Creek at the bottom, which runs to the southward to join the river Monongahela, twelve miles above its confluence with the Allegheny; we then descended another hill by an equally bad and dangerous road.   It is astonishing that in so fine and so improving a country more attention is not paid to the roads.   A turnpike is projected from Pittsburg to Harrisburg, which I am clearly of opinion might be kept in repair by a reasonable toll; and then wagons with goods may travel between the two places in a third less time than they do now, and without the present great risks of breaking down, and the mails may be delivered at the post offices one-half sooner.

"When about seven miles from Pittsburgh we had a picturesque view of the Monongahela on the left, which was soon hid again by the intervening hills, and then within three miles of that town the view was beautiful over the low cultivated level, or bottom as it is called, which skirts the river Allegheny from thence to Pittsburgh, which is seen at the confluence of that river with the Monongahela; beyond which, the high and steep coal hill crowned by a farm house most romantically situated, seems to impend directly over the glass manufactory, on the bank of the river opposite the town. The last two miles was along the fine level above mentioned, passing on the right, between the road and the Allegheny, the handsome seat of Mr. John Woods, a respectable lawyer, and immediately after we passed Fort Fayette, a stockaded post on the right, entered Pittsburgh and put up at Wm. M'Cullough's excellent inn."

In 1805 the post and stages were running regularly to Pittsburgh from Chambersburg. In 1806 the turnpike road over the mountains was begun, and the road from Lancaster to Columbia, or Wright's Ferry, was completed. Philip Gossler kept the tavern and ran the ferry in 1800, and it is written that sometimes one hundred and fifty Pitt teams were awaiting to be ferried over the broad Susquehanna. The great ferry boat carried two Conestoga wagons and their teams at a time across the big placid river. In 1812 the ferry was replaced by the longest bridge in the world.

Turnpikes were also built from Columbia to York, and to Gettysburg and Chambersburg. In 1815 a slate and limestone road twenty-two feet wide was built between Bedford and Stoyestown, and the next year it was continued on to Greensburg.

A Conestoga wagon built in Middletown, Pennsylvania, in 1813, which belongs to the collection of historical vehicles owned by the Baltimore and Ohio Railroad Company. This wagon took part in their great centenary pageant, The Fair of the Iron Horse, which was presented at Baltimore, September 24 to October 8, 1927. By courtesy of Mr. F. X. Milholland, Assistant to the Senior Vice President, of the Baltimore and Ohio Railroad Company.

CHAPTER VII

Of the Conestoga Wagon and its Construction

MR. LANDIS has written a description of the wagon and something of its construction from the many that he has examined. He says: "Long before the wagon was ordered the wheelwright had gone into the forest and selected trees that would serve his purpose;

A Conestoga Wagon belonging to the Ford Museum at Dearborn, Michigan. This is complete and shows the removable sideboards in place.

The excessive overhang front and back not only kept out rain and dust, but brought the load nearer the horses. It also gave smartness to the outfit, for was it not the day of poke bonnets?

white oak for the framing, gum for the hubs, hickory for the axle trees and single trees, and poplar for the boards. Since the wooden parts of the wagon were made as light as practicable, the wood had to be as strong as possible, and no knots, checks, soft spots or unseasoned wood was permitted. The material and design of the wagon made it unbreakable under the trying conditions met with on roads full of ruts and rocks, and sometimes stumps and roots; on corduroy and log roads, through swamps, and on side hill roads that put a severe strain on the wheels on one side; therefore both the material and the workmanship had to be of the best. The trees were taken to the saw mill, for there were water-driven saw mills in the Conestoga country at an early day, and sawed into square pieces, planks, and boards cut to the proper length and ranked in an open shed, so that each layer crossed the preceding one, and there was an air space around each piece. The gum blocks for hubs were cut to length for a hub and the bark was generally not removed.

"Black or sour gum was used for the hubs. It is not a strong wood, nor does it work easily, but its fiber is interwoven and will not split.

The right side of the Conestoga wagon owned by Amos Gingrich, Lancaster, Pennsylvania. Photograph by the U. S. National Museum.

All of the wheelwrights in this country used it. In England and France they used twisted elm. All the wood was examined as it was twice re-ranked, and in three years some of it could be used. The spokes were split from straight white oak. The felloes were roughly sawed or shaped with an adz before seasoning and the wagon maker at odd times often roughly dressed down the spokes and other parts to facilitate drying. There was no royal road to avoid labor for the wagon maker. His trade was governed by tradition and he took pride in his work. Each mortise was a tight fit; corners which added weight and not strength were pared down and beveled; one piece was exactly like its counterpart on the other side of the wagon; although spokes were fashioned from split pieces by hand there was no apparent difference between them; where two pieces came together, the fit was perfect and the curves symmetrical. This careful workmanship had much to do with the admiration the wagon received when it rolled down the road with the eyes of its world upon it. It won the admiration of the wagoner, as it crashed through apparently impassable places without a creaking from its frame or a snap from its iron bands.

A Conestoga Wagon in the "Fair of the Iron Horse," presented by the B. & O. R. R. in 1927. Photograph by courtesy of The U. S. National Museum.

"Centuries of development are back of the wagon wheel of today, for a solid wheel supported the first ox or donkey cart of primitive times just as it does our automobiles. Over a century ago large wheels on carts and wagons were common; great, powerful and ponderous, they battered rough paths into roads, and behind the sturdy oxen and heavy draught horses led the way to progress and a wider

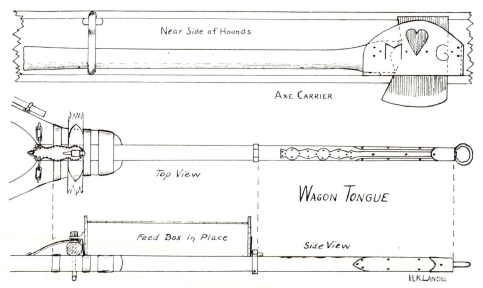

civilization, and like 'Old Man River' he keeps a-rollin', he jes keeps rollin' along. Strength requires that the load be supported upon vertical spokes; but the side thrust upon the wheel would soon fold it up like an umbrella if it were not designed to resist this. The spokes are therefore directed outward and are held in place by the heavy tire. The distance out from the spoke end at the hub, that the tire is moved, is called the 'dish.' Furthermore, the pressure of the loaded axle inside of the hub must be on a horizontal surface to keep the wheel from sliding out and bearing too hard against the linch pin. Since the axle is conical in shape and the bottom of it is horizontal, the plane of the wheel is inclined outward. The dish measures from two to three inches, depending on the size of the wheel,

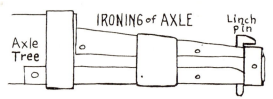

Drawings by H. K. Landis from originals at the Landis Valley Museum.

one-half inch per foot of the diameter. To make a good wheel required both skill and good material, for it is the vital part of a wagon. With the wheel the wagon stands or falls, so that it was made stronger than would appear necessary. The spokes were worked down with a hand axe, placed in a vise and further

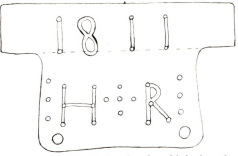

Forward hounds band. One-third size of original. Drawing from the original by H. K. Landis.

shaped with a draw knife and finished with a spoke shave. Perhaps a wooden caliper or gauge was used occasionally, but the workman usually depended upon his eye. A template or pattern helped in getting the proper shape and slant to the end that entered the mortise in the hub. The hub had been turned on a lathe and cored to receive the axle. The mortises were exactly placed and made so that the spokes had to be driven into them with powerful blows of the maul or sledge. They had to be in line and properly spaced at the outer end, for they could not be sprung very much; in fact, not at all with the shorter spokes of the front wheel. The end of the spoke was then accurately measured and sawed around and the tenon going into the felloe made by hand, sometimes round, but often square.

"The felloe was made in sections, two spokes to a section, dowelled at the ends. When in place the ends had to fit perfectly, and a crook in the felloe might mean a broken wheel

1   3   4   2

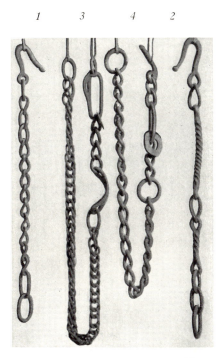

Nos. 1 and 2 are stay chains. Nos. 3 and 4 are Rough Locks, from the collection of The Landis Valley Museum.

It is not until you have actually seen and handled these chains with their hand-forged links which were made in such infinite variety, that you can appreciate the excellence of the craftsmanship of these Americans, who put so much of beauty as well as strength in their work.

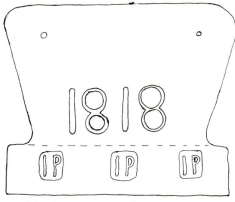

After hounds band. One-half size of original. Drawing from the original by H. K. Landis.

later. The ends of the spokes were wider apart than the inside mortises meant to fit them, so they were drawn together by a special tool and driven in until the felloe rested squarely upon the square shoulder of the tenon. The outer side of the felloe was naturally square with the spoke, and the tire had to rest flat upon the road. Owing to the dish of the wheel, which was necessary to give it lateral strength, the inner edge of the felloe had a greater diameter than the outer edge and this had to be adjusted by expanding the inner edge of the tire. Probably a compromise was effected, the wagon maker paring down a little and the blacksmith expanding a little, so that one edge of the tire might not be too thin.

"When the hub was provided with iron bands on both sides of the line of spokes, with a sleeve at both ends and an iron box or bushing inside, it was ready for the tire.

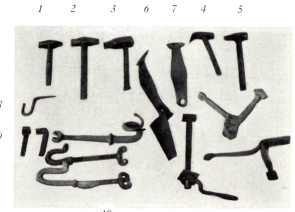

Nos. 1, 2, 3, 4, and 5 are hammer-headed double tree pins. No. 8 is a staple hook for a brake cahin. No. 9 is a pair of linch pins. No. 10 shows three stay chain hooks. Nos. 6 and 7 are double tree latches. Landis Valley Museum.

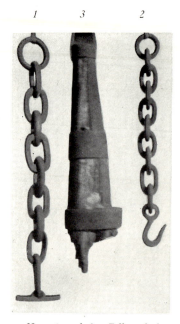

Nos. 1 and 2—Felloe chains for rough lock. No. 3—Ironing of axle, top to the right. Landis Valley Museum.

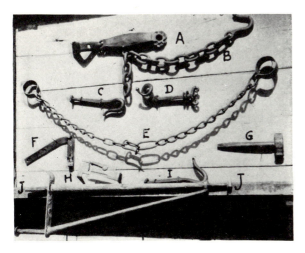

Conestoga Wagon. Details from the Landis Valley Museum. A—Double tree link for pin G. B—Stay chain, ring held by hooks C or D. C, D, I—Stay chain, hooks of two shapes. E—Spread chain for wagon bed. F—Latch to fasten middle of end gate. G—Wagon hammer or double tree pin. The iron handle is used as a double tree pin: the chisel end, to raise the lynch pin· H— Ax socket with latch. J—Side brace for side of wagon bed. Landis Valley Museum.

The inside sleeve projected far over the end of the hub to prevent sand and dust from falling upon the axle. The same was done with the outer sleeve, but there was also cut into its edge a rectangular notch through which the linch pin could be lifted when the wheel was to be removed. There was also a long narrow slot near the edge opposite this notch, into which the hub cover hooked, being fastened by a staple on the opposite side, and having a plug to fit in the linch pin notch. These covers kept the sand and dust out of the outer end of the axle.

"The first wagon tires used in this country were made of short pieces of iron, since longer ones were not available, the length of a section of felloe, butting at the middle of the felloe to bind the joint. But the iron industry progressed quickly, so that all the Conestoga tires we have examined have two welds, single bars long enough to

Model, scale three-quarters of an inch equals one foot, based on original wagon owned by Amos Gingrich, Lancaster, Pennsylvania. Model by Paul E. Garber, of the U. S. National Museum staff. Made for the Pennsylvania Railroad exhibit at the Sesquicentennial, 1926. Wagon, accurate harness, from a painting, unauthenticated.

One of the largest Conestoga wagons in existence, now belonging to Mr. John Orndorff, of Littlestown. This wagon was built in 1823 for Mr. John Small, of Franklin County, by a wheelwright named Zentmyer, and ironed by a blacksmith named Cromer.

It was first used to carry coal from Williamsport to Chambersburg. The second generation of the Small family used it for freighting, principally to and from Baltimore, while the third generation used it as a farm wagon.

reach half way around the wheel having been used. It was heavy work handling a hundred and fifty pounds for welding in a brick forge hearth, on a small anvil to the tune of quick-moving sledges, on a bending roll, and kneading one edge to make it longer, but they did it. Then came the great day when the tire was laid out flat on iron or stone supports and a fire built around it until it was quite hot (hot enough to char wood); then it was lifted on to the wheel lying horizontally upon a buck, and quickly driven over the felloe and as quickly quenched with pouring water. Cooling was completed in a cooling trough, in which the wheel hung and revolved. All the neighborhood would come to watch the shrinking of the tire, for the flames and smoke, the hurry of hammering, the volumes of hissing steam, were a fine sight.

"To make the fit tight the blacksmith had measured the circumference of the wooden wheel and taken off one and one-half inches to get the inner circumference of the tire, and cut the iron accordingly. This measuring was done with a traveler, a wooden or iron wheel rolling along the surface and provided with a handle, and a piece of

Putting the cover on the Conestoga wagon, which was built in 1823 for Mr. John Small, of Franklin County. Mrs. Mary Secrist Small spun the flax for this cover and for the teamster's mattress for this wagon.

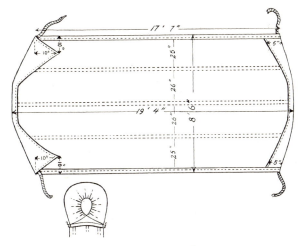

The inside of the old hempen homespun wagon cover, showing the turn in at either end, to allow the draw string to give the right shape to the openings. Drawing by H. K. Landis.

chalk. Rectangular holes had been punched in the tire opposite the ends of the spokes, and into these were driven wedges or pins made by the smith to exactly fit the holes, and designed to keep the tire from sliding sidewise, when it became loosened.

"The axle and axletree were made from the strongest wood available, white oak or hickory; the bottom edge was horizontal and the top edge inclined eight or nine degrees to it, making a conical axle two and three-quarters inches in diameter at the outer end and five inches in diameter at the inner end of the sixteen and three-quarter-inch cone. There was a flush band of iron one and one-half inches broad around the outer end and another two and three-quarters inches broad around the middle, holding the top and bottom wearing plates of the axle in place; the inner end of the top plate was held by strong spikes and the end of the lower plate passed under the two-inch band around the six-inch axle tree. To the top of the latter band was riveted on the inside an iron block, against which the inside hub box pressed while the outer hub box wore against the linch pin, or against a thick ring when the wear became excessive. Sometimes a heavy wearing ring was placed at the inside end of the axle. The linch pin was square, with the top bent outward, so that it could be lifted out with the chisel end of the iron wagon hammer. Thus the axle was almost encased in iron and protected against the hammering of the hub, sliding back and forth, that could be heard far away.

"The axle tree was gracefully shaped and rounded and above it the bolster was made to correspond. They carried hooks that held the tar box and water bucket, and between them passed the rear hounds fastened with ornate pins, and the coupling pole. They were bolted together with heavy flush-top bolts with single wing nuts on the lower ends.   The axle tree and wheels were the parts most frequently replaced, because of the great strain upon them.   A short wooden standard, and later an iron one, was placed in the outer ends of the bolster to keep the wagon bed from slipping off sidewise.   On the forward side of this bolster was the rocker bar of the side brake, held by two eye bolts.   The brake lever was held by a screw nut to the squared end of this bar; at the center of the bolster was a short crank welded to the rocker bar, pinned to a connecting rod, leading to the brake beam, and often stiffened by spreading iron braces.   On the end of the brake beam were the rubbing blocks, often faced with the soles of old boots and held by inward turned cleats.   The lever was operated by a long chain and could be fastened down by passing one of its links over a pin on the forward edge of the brake beam, about the middle of the rubbing block.   These pins were made in various shapes, as was also the small hook on the side of the wagon bed, on which to hang the end of the brake chain when not in use.   The blacksmiths took delight in fancifully shaping these small hooks.

"The front axle tree was similar in shape to the rear one, but the bolster had no standard and was sloped up to the middle, where rested the rubbing plate or grease bench, through which the king pin passed. On the forward hounds, which passed between the axle tree and bolster, was an iron frame, the top of which was level with the top of the bolster, and upon which the bed block rubbed when canted through turning the wagon.   The front axle tree also carried the stay chain hooks, ornate ironwork resembling a coiled snake, or a snake with head drawn back, eyes punched in and mouth indicated, but not open.   As the front wheel was seldom over four feet high, the wing nuts below the axle tree were not over twenty inches from the road, and that is one reason why the wheel was not made low enough to pass under the bed when turning; another reason was the much greater pull that was necessary to roll a smaller wheel over rough surfaces, for the wagoner was always considerate of his horses.   From the front and through the rear carriages passed a coupling pole inserted between the bolsters and axle trees, fastened in front by the king pin running through it and passing freely through the rear · carriage as far back as the bed extended.   The rear hounds extended forward above the pole and met in a flat iron-bound plate fastened loosely to it by a band, through which passed a headed pin. There were several holes through the coupling pole at this place, to allow the wagon to be lengthened or shortened as desired. On the rear hounds were various devices in which the brake beam slid back and forth, although a plain raised iron frame, sometimes S-shaped, was generally preferred. Since the hounds were placed at an angle and the brake beam slid straight back and forth, the edge of the guide had to be parallel to the pole, in order to bear upon the pins in the beam; and bringing the ends of the guides back to the pole again for fastening, naturally made a reverse curve. The hounds terminated just back of the bolster and were mortised in, bolted and held behind by an ornate iron pin, flattened above into a large heart or tulip or circle, pierced by two nail holes. The forward hounds were also mortised in and bolted, but extended backward, and the ends were joined by a rubbing strip or 'reibscheit' which was ironed on top, passing under the pole, which here bore an iron plate. As the rubbing plate, turning track or frame and rubbing piece, were in continual use, they had to be greased frequently, and wagoners spoke of this part as the grease bed. The front hounds were brought together on either side of the wagon tongue in a long joint and held there by a wooden pin and several broad iron bands. The forward of these bands was broad on top and sometimes carried the date and initials of the owner. I have never seen any maker's marks, but owner's initials are common, no doubt for identification. About a foot from the rear end of the tongue was a hole through the band, through which the all-iron wagon hammer handle passed to hold the double tree. A hasp was fastened by hinge or hook to the after end of the tongue and ran to the top of the double tree, the hammer pin passing through it, to take part of the pulling strain. The hasp was frequently ornamented and sometimes carried date and initials. The stay chains, which held the double tree from swinging too far either way, often had ornamented hooks in one end of them, and sometimes were of double twisted links.

"Since the wood was pared down to a compromise between strength and lightness, it was reenforced at every point of strain by ironing. The double tree was almost covered with iron, as were the ends of the tongue and the hubs. All rubbing surfaces were iron, covered or provided with iron rubbing plates. All accessories were ironed except the tar box; the jockey sticks that held the forward pairs of horses apart were wound with iron spirally wrapped, corners were iron protected, and the hinges and hasp of the tool box almost completely covered the lid, and thin iron bands the sides. The designs in this ornamental iron work were cut out with chisels and not filed, and this required skillful handling and beating out to the right thickness. Much could be said of this decorative work; of the persistence of the heart, tulip, snake and knob end motives; the painstaking symmetry of tapering double link hold back chains; the graceful turning of hooks and ingenious design of axe sockets and gate latches and spread chain fastening that prevented the spreading of the top of the bed; but that is another story.

"The frame and floor beams of the wagon bed or box were of white oak and the boards of poplar. The frame was mortised and wooden pinned except where the boards were fastened by rivets with square washers. On the inside of the bed iron strips ran up and down along the line of the frame studding and the rivets passed through these, with flat heads at the other end. This left the inside surface without obstructions to damage the freight and held the boards in place permanently. Nothing but a saw or an axe could remove one of those three-quarter inch poplar boards. The boards ran lengthwise in the bed; later they were placed crosswise on the floor for certain uses only. The frame was beveled and rounded everywhere to lighten it, but it was securely fastened together with corner bands of intricate shape, braces and knees. On the outside of the bed the bottom crossbeams at the rear end and in the middle extend beyond the side of the bed, and iron braces resting upon them prevent the sides from being pushed outward by the load. This is further accomplished by three pairs of spread chains fastened at their middle by a slip-ring catch, both novel and effective. The braces mentioned consist of three parts; a vertical tapered rod bolted through the beam and a diagonal taper brace bolted below and with a sliding eye end, which permits the side of the bed to move inward but not outward. The front end of the box is permanently fastened by corner plates and pins; the bottom of it curves downward and the top upward at the middle of the end, and near the end of the top rail are hooks or rings fastening the heavy drawing cord of the front of the cover, which pulls it together, allowing only about a foot or so of opening. The cords are not tied together, but pass to the ring on the opposite side of the end. No one sits at the front of the bed, as they would in a prairie schooner, moving wagon or Southern covered wagon or military supply wagon. The rear end gate has downward projecting vertical frames, which slip into staples in the end frame of the bottom, and holes in the sidewise projecting top frame slip over the rounded ends of the upper gate rail, to be fastened by a pin hanging by a chain. The middle rails of end and sides are fastened by latches provided with hasp and hook. It may be explained that the side framing consists of a rounded top piece, a larger bottom piece and a small middle stringer. Across these pass the upright pieces framed into the horizontal pieces and forming two rows of rectangular panels all around the body. Staples on the sides of the bed are provided for the side boards and hoops.

"The Civil War covered wagons, the covered wagons and carts of the South and the prairie schooner were all built with a straight box-like body instead of the curved boat-shaped one of the true Conestoga, whose bottom was also curved crosswise. The bottoms of the late ore and pig-iron wagons were also straight and flat. The first iron works in Pennsylvania began operation about 1718 and was closely followed by similar enterprises, so that in 1728 there were four blast furnaces in operation. Baron Stiegel built his furnace in 1757. In 1786 there were seventeen furnaces, forges and slitting mills within thirty miles of Lancaster; in 1805 there were in Lancaster County three furnaces and eight forges, each producing twelve hundred tons a year; in 1838 there were within fifty-two miles of Lancaster one hundred and two furnaces, forges and rolling mills; and the Conestoga wagon did most of the hauling for these. Also, the surplus of the countryside had to be taken to the Philadelphia and Baltimore markets, the grain converted into alcohol and whiskey, the fruit into cider and vinegar, the wheat into flour, and flaxseed into linseed oil; all of these things, as well as pottery, glassware and tobacco, were packed in barrels or casks for shipping. There were four and five cask wagons.

"The excessive overhang at both ends of the wagon, reminiscent of the poke bonnets of the period, was quite as fashionable, but it also kept out rain and dust, and made a much larger load possible than could have been carried had the ends been straight, and a longer bed was impossible as the wagon could not have been turned had the wheels been more than twelve feet apart.

"I think the painting of Conestoga wagons was the result of conditions, rather than any aesthetic preference, although the Amish today have a decided liking for light blue, pink and cherry red. In the earlier days there were not many colors available. All new woodwork on the running part of any wagon was given its first coat of red by the wagon maker and this is done to this day. It is a very serviceable and desirable color, although it has to be ground just before using in a hand paint mill. This did not apply to carriages and sulkys, but to all farm apparatus, such as plows, harrows, etc. Black was the favorite color for carriages and yellow for sleighs, with black stripes. Red lead is a bright vermilion, but cherry red was often used for household cupboards and chairs and for things in the barn, like fanning mills, hay ladders, horse powers, etc. Blue was used less frequently, but mostly the wagon bodies were thus painted. The forebay walls and gates were sometimes blue and also the wall of the porch. Sometimes blued white-wash was used. Today, when you see a blue yard gate at the home of an Amish family, it means there is a marriageable daughter there. Indigo was used by every family in washing, and so they always had blue for their whitewash. As to the custom regarding the older wagons, say before 1800, we have no evidence to the contrary. All the old wagons we have examined were thus painted and we found no wagon with an undercoat of a different color. When you have said red, blue, yellow and black you have the color vocabulary of colonial days in this section. Of course, all the harness and iron was black, the wagon was vermilion, the body light indigo, the side boards red and the cover white. The wagon jack was red, the tar box black, the feed box blue and the bucket either red or unpainted. Buckets had the name of the owner painted upon their sides and his initials and the date were put in iron upon the wagon jack.

"The English wagon bore its owner's name and the name of his home, on a board on the near side. In America this was almost never done, though the owner's initials were sometimes marked in the iron work near the date. But the Conestoga wagons greatly surpassed the English ones in their decorative iron work and their accessories.

"Paint came in barrels in those days and had to be broken up before it could be used, just as sugar cones did. The English used priming coats before they applied red lead, but wagon makers here dug up the firm red lead, placed it on the rubbing stone with good linseed oil and rubbed until it was smooth. The paint had to be used at once, for it soon settled solidly at the bottom of the earthenware paint pot and refused to be stirred up. Prussian blue also came in solid form and had to be ground in oil by the expenditure of much perspiration and persistence. But when put on, these paints stuck.

"The white wagon cover of hempen homespun fitted over broad hickory hoops, fastened into iron sockets or staples on the outside of the body. The lowest bows were midway between the ends, and the others rose gradually in a deep curve to front and rear, so that the ends were of nearly equal height. The cover was corded down on the sides and drawn together by draw ropes at the ends, so that the wagon was almost closed in.

"Last week we acquired a wagon cover of hemp, torn and worn, but complete. It shows worn strips, indicating eight hoops, and is made of four pieces of hemp cloth, lap sewn, with an inch hem along the sides, and folded at the ends, to allow the draw string to give the right shape to the opening. When the wagon load was not a heavy one, it was piled up to the top of the cover, and the side boards held it in. These were boards placed on the top rail of the bed and held there by cleats passing downward through broad staples on the outside of the bed. The bed being curved, the bottom of the side board was shaped to fit it, but the top was straight. The cover was stretched over hoops, eight for the ordinary farm wagon, and as many as twelve for the later wagons that carried freight over the turnpike roads. These hoops were split from a log with a frow, and it was a delicate operation, as they had to be of an even width and thickness and not jointed. The surface was smoothed with a draw knife and the ends tapered to fit into the staples on the side of the bed. The hoops were lined up at the top by a spacing strip. Later, some of the covers may have been made of flax tow, and when cotton cloth came in, of canvas; the Conestoga was always loaded and emptied at its rear end."

CHAPTER VIII

Of Conestoga Wagon Iron by H. K. Landis

THE only real evidence we have as to dates in connection with the Conestoga wagon are the dates found on the old iron. When a wagon was broken up, the iron was used on a new wagon, so that the wagon itself is no absolute indication, or rather, the iron does not always tell the age of the wagon on which one today finds it. But it does tell when the iron part was made. Yesterday (May 18, 1929) we went to two public sales and found nothing, so we stopped at Clay, at one of the old hotels, and took some photographs, talked awhile with Old Man Elser about hemp mills, and then the local blacksmith came along and invited us over to his shop. Before that

Hub end covers for sandy roads, to keep the dust from the axles. Landis Valley Museum. See page 67.

he had asked what the earliest date we had on Conestoga iron was, and we told him 1803. He said he had one, 1811. "Let us see your wagon jacks," we said, and he showed us one dated 1814, another 1852, and then one of 1770, and another, which we bought, of 1782. Then he took us out in the shop yard and we looked over tons of old iron and wagons, buying two axe sockets, four hound pins, and a complete wagon tongue with two date pieces on it of 1863. He had a hub end cover he would not sell, but we bought several serpent head stay chain hooks.

When the blacksmith ironed the wagon he put the date upon it occasionally — not always. He had straight and curved chisels, which he easily made himself and tempered, and with several sizes of these and a circular punch he was able to make designs that are legible today, notwithstanding the rust and wear of generations. The letters on the hounds bands were large and on the wagon jacks

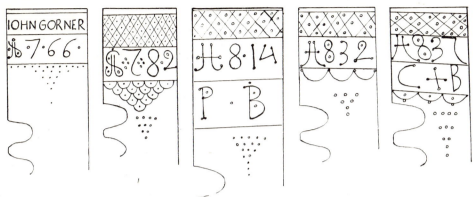

Wagon jack inscriptions, showing the date and initials or name of owner.
Drawings by H. K. Landis, from the originals in the Landis Valley Museum.

the date occupied the width of the rack or pillar. None of these dates were scratched or scribed, all were punched or cut with a chisel and hammer.

1 — The "one" as it invariably appears on Conestoga wagons and nowhere else.
2 — Another variation of the numeral "one" in iron. This form Mr. Landis thinks means A. D.
3 — The numeral "one" as it appears on chests, date stones, etc., standing for Jahr.
*   The form with the dot above and the fork below is the first stage in the development and is found*
*   between 1742 and 1764.*

There is invariably an indiscriminate use of the letter I and J and the numeral one in communities of German descent. The single J for one stands for Jahr, and is common on chests, date stones, etc. Sometimes, as on old cast stove plates, the curve of the J is extended, making the monogram "a. d. I." The double I crossed, we have found only on Conestoga iron, and I think it means "Jahr Herr Jesu," or year of our Lord Jesus. The reversal of the J does not seem to have special significance. On the jacks at Clay we saw for the first time a variation of the double J crossed, and the one we bought resembles those found on some stove or fire-

Conestoga wagon dates in iron, from the Landis Valley Museum, Lancaster. H. K. Landis thinks that the odd form of the one may possibly stand for Jahr Herr Jesu, or year of our Lord.

place plates. (See "The Bible in Iron," by Dr. H. C. Mercer.)

To tar the axles, the jack was placed under the axletree near the wheel and the wheel was raised just free of the ground; the linch pin was taken out and the hub drawn out until the inner box of the hub rested on the end of the axle; then the tar

Conestoga Wagon Jacks, dated 1766, 1814 and 1832. Lancaster County, Pennsylvania.

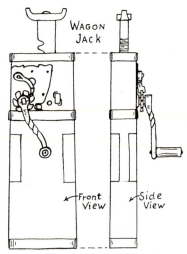

Landis Valley Museum.   Sketch.

was smeared on with a paddle, and the hub pushed back into place. A load of three or four tons required that the jack be sturdy and readily handled. The fact that jacks bearing dates of a century and a half ago are still in use, testifies to their excellence of design and material. The jack dated 1782 has a 6.5-inch crank and two revolutions raise the load one tooth, or .8-inch. To raise half a ton would require a pressure of at least twenty pounds on the crank, through the manipulation of a 6.5-inch crank, a 4-tooth pinion, a 24-tooth wheel, a 3-gear pinion and a rack. The wear on some of these old wagon jacks (the oldest in the Landis Valley Museum is 1766) indi-

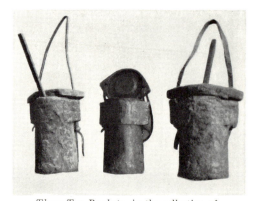

Three Tar Buckets, in the collection of The Landis Valley Museum. See pages 79 and 80.

cates frequent use. Wagon jacks at first and for many years were made by the blacksmith who ironed the wagon. Generally they had two spurs in the base to prevent their slipping, a wooden body, a riveted together or keyed gear case, a ratchet wheel on the crank, a strong geared pillar with turntable two-spur top. As they were very necessary to a team on the road, the owner's name or initials were put on the top of the pillar, with the date.

A wagon jack dated 1762, in the Ford Museum at Dearborn, has no ratchet and pawl, but a ring

Wagon Jack, dated 1762. From The Henry Ford Historical Museum, Dearborn, Mich.

or hook holds the handle when the jack is up. The wagon jack was hung from the inside

Tar box, two feed or water buckets and axe socket for Conestoga wagons. Landis Valley Museum.

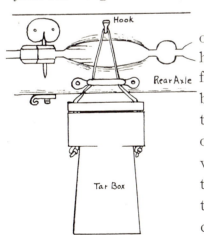

Landis Valley Museum. Sketch.

of the front hounds or from the back axletree, by its own contrivance. The tar pot or teer lodel contained pine tar for

Ornate Tarpot Hook. Below it on the axletree is a staple six inches wide, through which the leather strap passes, before being hung over the hook shown, to prevent swaying about. See pages 69, 78, 80 and 86.

lubricating the axles and the grease bed.   The box cover fitted over a dust-proof edge and often had a hole in the middle, through which the paddle was stuck, though sometimes the slot was in the edge of the cover or the side of the box.   It was slung under the rear axle tree by a leather handle.

The bucket was turned on a lathe from a small tree, leaving ears at the upper end, through which the leather handle passed.   Lard was sometimes added to the tar in cold weather.   Tar was plentiful and came from the Carolina turpentine camps, packed in high, narrow casks, and had many uses on a farm.

Arriving at the stopping place for the night, either a wagoner's inn or wagon stand, or at the side of the road if the inns were overcrowded, the feed box was unslung from the rear end gate, and placed on the wagon tongue.   One end had a flat projecting iron at the bottom, which slid into a staple on the tongue; the other end had a projecting piece with a hole in it.   The wagon hammer was lifted, the doubletree passed back, and the hole placed over the hole in the tongue, inserting the wagon hammer to hold it, Into this huge feed box, longer than the wagon was wide, the feed for the horses was placed and, after removing the harness, they were tied within reach of the box to eat their fill.   The traveling farmer carried his own feed, but the professional wagoner bought his where he stopped.   After breakfast, at daylight the next morning, the box was returned to its place at the rear end, where it hung like a bustle, sheltered by the projecting cover and sometimes holding the feed in bags for the next stop. The horses were watered

A Conestoga tool box lid in the Pennsylvania Museum in Fairmount Park.   This lid is supposed to be nearly two hundred years old.

The heart and tulip design on a Conestoga tool box cover. Courtesy of the Antiquarian Magazine.

from the water bucket that hung at the rear axletree on the pole or on the side of the wagon bed. They rested on their bedding of straw, out under the stars, while their driver boasted of them in the bar room of the inn.

Much might be written about the ironing of the lid of the Conestoga wagon tool box. There was an early use and knowledge of iron in the province of Pennsylvania. The smith was an honored personage who shaped the traditions of the old world and the lore of the Black Forest in what he made, and his decorations of these old boxes are an unfailing delight. Some are almost covered with ornate ironwork, symmetrical, uniform and strongly riveted; for the box was of light boards and could be badly broken. Today they sell for more than a farmer has to pay for a modern farm wagon. Such is the way of art. The staples of the hinges were driven through the top rail and clinched. The hasp fitted over a staple and could be fastened by

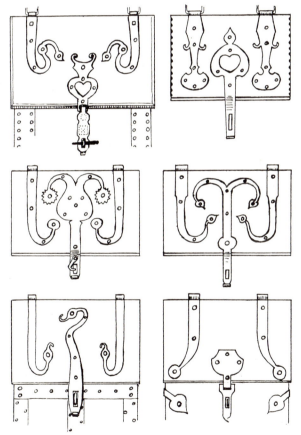

Tool Box Lids. The Landis Valley Museum.

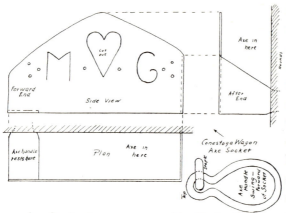

Axe Carrier from wagon owned by Clayton Groff,
near Eden, Pa. See pages 64 and 71.

a hook or a padlock. On the more recent farm Conestogas, tool boxes are found on the middle of the front end, but these are more or less in the way, for the horses were hitched as close to the wagon as possible. These front boxes are smaller than the old side ones, as these farm wagons rarely went very great distances. In the side tool boxes was everything for an emergency — pincers, tongs, wrench, bolts, nails, open links, straps, etc.

There was also a pleasing variation of axe sockets, though we know of only two style of axe handle ring supports. Few sockets are decorated, but they take many shapes and sometimes there is a latch to keep the axe from jumping out on a rough road. The ends of the sockets were driven into the hounds or nailed with hand-forged rose-headed nails. The axes had straight hickory handles, worked down with a draw knife, and were of the pole and bit type; if the wagon were mired or a strip or corduroy road had to be built the axe was a necessary and sufficient tool. A modern wagon might carry a hatchet, but everything about the Conestoga was on a large scale. Great strength was necessary to resist great

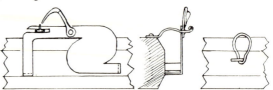

Axe Socket, Conestoga wagon of Sam'l Gingrich,
Lancaster

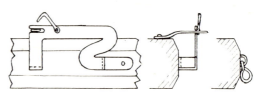

Axe Socket, Conestoga wagon of Stehman Farm,
Long Lane

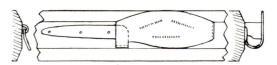

Axe Socket, Conestoga wagon of G. K. Herr,
Millersville, Pennsylvania
Drawings from the originals by H. K. Landis

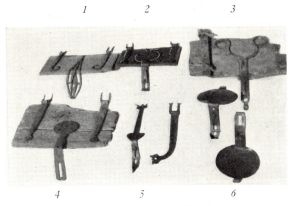

Nos. 1, 2, 3, 4, and 5—Tool Box Lids, showing ornamental hinges and locks. No. 6—Hub End Covers. Landis Valley Museum.

strain. They swarmed over a vast and rich countryside for more than a century and rumbled on to still wider fields. They dealt with primitive forces in a primitive way, and pulled through.

Very early in the development of wagons it was found that the width of tire and its diameter had much to do with the horse power required to pull the wagon. This was given undue importance, resulting in wheels of unusual size and supposed adaptability to either soft or hard roads. An example of the extremes which a lack of actual tests produced, was the toll schedule of the Philadelphia Lancaster Turnpike Company, dated 1792. Having built the first turnpike in the country, and a very fine one (sixty-four and a half miles, at a cost of $6,200 per mile — the stock was sold at public cry, and is said to have been the beginning of our stock exchange), they meant to keep it in good condition. A two-wheeled sulky with one horse paid a levy a ten-mile section; a wagon with four wheels and two horses a shilling; or with four horses two levys. Then follows the strange pronouncement: For every cart or wagon whose

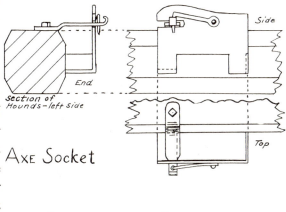

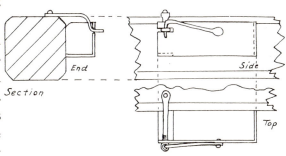

Drawings by H. K. Landis, from originals at the Landis Valley Museum. See page 82.

Tool box and side of wagon, detail.   National Geographic Society.   Reproduced by special permission from The National Geographic Magazine.

wheels do not exceed the breadth of four inches, one levy for each horse drawing the same. For wheels which exceed in breadth four inches, and not seven inches, one fip or half levy or sixteenth of a dollar. For a width of tire between seven and ten inches, or being the breadth of 7 inches shall roll 10 inches, five cents for every horse drawing the same. For 10 to 12-inch tires rolling over 15 inches, three cents. For wheels with tires over 12 inches wide, two cents per horse per ten-mile section or fraction thereof. Further, between December first and May first, no team with tires less than

TRIP LATCH for BED CHAIN   Six of these links — then the twisted links

4 inches may be loaded over two and one-half tons; from 4 to 7 inches, three and one-half tons; from 7 to 10 inches, five tons; during the remainder of the year the limit was about one-half a ton more per wagon. Then comes an unusual prohibition, relating to loaded vehicles, requiring all with tires less than 9 inches wide to be drawn by not more than six horses, while no team might have more than eight; failing in which, one of the horses was to be confiscated for the use of the company charging tolls, two oxen or one mule were equivalent to one horse. In his "Wayside Inns on the Lancaster Roadside," Julius Sachse wrote:

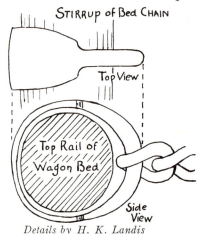

STIRRUP of BED CHAIN

Top View

Top Rail of Wagon Bed

Side View

Details by H. K. Landis

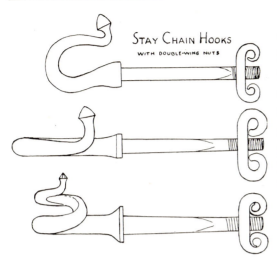

Stay Chain Hooks
WITH DOUBLE-WING NUTS

*Drawings by H. K. Landis, from originals in
The Landis Valley Museum.*

"On the new road, broad-wheeled wagons, such as were known by the name of Conestogas, Turnpike Schooners, or Pitt Teams, were supposed to carry thirty barrels of flour or three tons; the usual freight charged was one dollar per barrel, while the toll between Philadelphia and Lancaster was three dollars or about a dollar a ton."

Later, there were two classes of tires; a narrow one, about two inches wide, an inch thick and perhaps six feet in diameter, for the rear wheel of the road wagon of the professional wagoner or regular; and a broad tire, four or five inches wide, three-quarters of an inch thick and five feet in diameter, for the farm wagons which were known as militia, when they carried frieght. Broad tires persisted because soft roads did. In 1804 the highway from Philadelphia to Baltimore was said to be in an execrable condition, and the width of tires was a subject for discussion for nearly a hundred years.

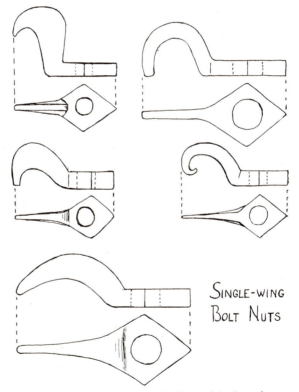

Single-wing
Bolt Nuts

*Drawings by H. K. Landis, from originals at the
Landis Valley Museum.*

The Pennsylvania State Board of Agriculture, 1891-1896, published information upon vehicular traction and factors affecting it, and giving the results of government tests, which proved that the pull required to haul the wagon decreases as the diameter of the wheel increases, but the rear wheel must not be so high as to make loading difficult, while the front wheel must be small enough to turn the wagon about.   It required 41.6 per cent as much power to pull a wagon with six-foot wheels and tires three inches wide over grass, as to do the same thing with tires half as wide. On a dirt road the advantage was 12.7 per cent.

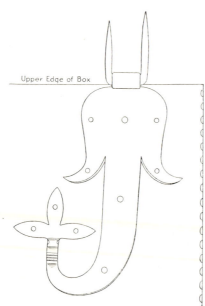

Upper Edge of Box

Outline sketch of Hinge on Wagon Box Lid.   Forged iron.

While the very high rear wheel had advantages on the road, it was not so good for the farm wagon, so that militia wagons were sometimes made with two sets of rear wheels, one pair six feet in diameter for the road and a pair five feet in diameter for the farm. Going back still farther, Mr. G. M. Weaver writes that his father, who made Conestoga wagons, spoke of "the practice of making wagons in his younger years with two sets of wheels —four high wheels with a narrow tread for long distance hauling, and four lower wheels with a wider tread, suitable for farm work and for hauling logs and lumber. I never heard of wheels higher than six feet for road work, and these had a three-inch tread; but for farm work a width of four or four and one-half inches was used," he adds.

A practical consideration influenced the width of tires, in the difficulty of adjusting the angle of the dish of the wheel to the horizontal road surface. The felloe was square with the spokes, but as the spokes above were at an angle with the vertical, the felloe face was conical and the tire had to fit it and be conical too. This was easy with a tire two inches wide, but with one measuring five and one-half inches, too much of one side of the tire had to be removed.

The blacksmith favored the narrow tire, which greatly influenced its general adoption on road wagons of Conestoga days and modern farm wagons. With smaller wheels and less dish, there was less difficulty and so the wide tires were generally used on the farms.

The Conestoga Wagon as it really was. This is the wagon belonging to Mr. Amos Gingrich, of Lancaster.

Whatever they may have tried to do in the eighteenth century, the general usage when wagoning was at its height was a four-inch tire east of the Alleghenies and narrower ones for the harder roads of the Pittsburgh section.

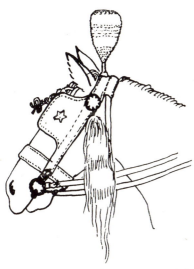

Fully-equipped headgear of a high-mettled Conestoga.

The blacksmith at Clay said he had some four-inch tires, but that they were of farm wagons. The road wagons had tires about two and one-half inches wide, perhaps an inch thick. This is on the road from Downington to Lebanon (Topton) and Harrisburg, and from there west. The road was hard and there was no penalty on narrow tires. Thus it seems that broad tires were needed principally on soft roads, but even then I have never seen them greater than four inches in width."

CHAPTER IX

Of the Conestoga Six-Horse Team and the Harness

THE harness, or gears, as it was called by the wagoners, was made by the village saddler of the Conestoga Valley. The leather was bark tanned, using oak bark, the work done by hand and the process requiring from eight to ten months. Leather cured in this way never loses its life and softness. The harness was cut and sewed by hand. The saddler sat astride his "horse" with pieces of leather held in a vise, and he sewed back and forth, using two waxed linen threads. The harness for the pole horses was heavier and was made differently from that of the other horses, having a heavy breeching, which helped control the pole and hold back the load. The neck of the horse collar and the hames were protected by a large piece of leather called a housing, held in place by being slipped over the end of the hames. Bridles were entirely of flat leather, and blinders were made of single pieces of leather, unstiffened. The driver used only one line to control the lead horse, which in turn controlled the whole team by means of the jockey stick. The jockey stick was a thin piece of seasoned hickory wood, wound or wrapped with leather bands for strength, and fastened to the hames of the lead horse and to the bit of his mate, the off horse. Particular attention was paid to the leather in the line. This had to be supple and smooth grained. The whip was of leather sewed to form a cylinder-like handle, which was filled solidly. The end tapered and was finished with a plaited leather cracker, and this was tipped with a plaited waxed thread. The saddle was a flat affair of three pieces of leather. The center was padded with straw and lined with a heavy coarse homespun material, either linen or cotton. Later ticking was used.*

The jerk line to the forward or lead horse was stronger on the road wagons than on those used by the farmers. It was made of heavy leather, well greased, with a slit in the after end, by which it was hung over the near hame, and the slack was looped about once or twice. The wagoner held the line, giving short jerks to turn the lead horse to the right, and a long pull to turn him to the left. This was helped by having the outside rein a little over an inch shorter

*W. deC. Ravenel, The United States National Museum, Washington, D. C.

than the inside one.   The lead rein was fastened to a ring into which
the jerk line was buckled.   The wagoner also talked to his horses,
and "haw" and "gee" meant "left "and "right" to Conestoga horses,
as they have to horses all over the country since those old days.
One old teamster would stand before his lead horse, Bill, and tell him
what was expected of him, and Bill would hang his head and point
his ears, and plainly promise to do his best.   But when they stopped
for breath at the top of a long hill, and he told them what good horses

*Interesting variations of the old wagon are to be found in different localities.   Mr. A. H.
Thuma of Boiling Springs, Cumberland County, has a very large wagon which was built about
1840 by a wheelwright named Abragast, whose shop was near Shippensburg.   It was ironed by a
Mr. Gipp with Simon Smith as his apprentice.   The coupling pole extends beyond the rear end
gate and is curved, to allow the teamster to use it for a support in loading, and barrels could be
rolled up the end of it.   The coupling pole also has an auxiliary coupling pin back of the rear
axle, so that in case the regular pin should break the wagon would not pull apart.   This wagon
has eleven bows and the roof, from the arch of the front bow to the arch of the last one, measures
twenty-two feet.   The top of the wagon bed is seventeen feet long, and the wagon has the reputation
of having hauled many a load of one hundred hundred-weight.   Mr. Thuma has hauled a load in
it in recent years weighing 13,865 pounds, and the empty wagon weighs 2,700 pounds.   This
wagon is complete with all the old harness and bells.   The hames are worked out of the wood of
white oak trees, selected because they had grown almost into shape.*

they were, they arched their necks and champed their bits proudly.
Although he cracked his whip fiercely, he was never seen to strike a
horse; and if he nodded in his saddle, at the end of a long day, his
team took him safely home.   The farm dog who slept in the stable
with the horses often followed the farm wagon on its long road
journeys, though the regular wagoners rarely had dogs.   The wheel
horses were usually the heaviest ones on the team and the most
dependable, for they not only pulled, but they turned the wagon and
backed it, as well.   The broad leather traces from the hames to the
tail were of double thickness and half a foot wide; they were supported
from a ring in the backing gear by a strap, and were continued to the
singletrees by short chain traces.   The backing gear over the horses

hips and behind his thighs was also broad and heavy, for when backing the wagon the horse threw his weight against it, and this pull was transmitted forward to the end of the tongue through the traces, breast chains and the backing chains, attached to the tongue ring. These breast chains were beautifully made with close twisted links, and there is in the Landis Valley Museum a pair of backing chains with double twisted links, evenly tapered from end to end. An ornamental rosette fastened the pendant colored hair tassel and a pompon stuck up between the ears on gala occasions, when the bridle and bell hoops were also wound with bright ribbons. It was a brave sight. The whip, eight or nine feet long, was unlike those used on stage coaches or private coaches, nor did drovers or the drivers of the later prairie schooners use this kind. It could be hung from the hames from a loop sometimes sewed on the side.

WAGONERS Whip
Leather

Sketch by H. K. Landis,
Landis Valley Museum

A spreader carrying singletrees at both ends was hooked into the tongue end ring, and to these the second pair of horses were hitched by all chain traces, covered with leather where they touched the ribs of the horses, and held up by a broad leather saddle piece. To prevent the singletrees rattling against the horses' heels, a strap passed from the hip to near the rear end of the trace to hold it up. The harness was much lighter than that for the wheel horses, and the jerk line passed through a brass ring in the top of the hames of the near horse.

The lead horses were the lightest of the team, and if there was any prancing to do, they did it. The near horse was the real leader, and the off horse, often an apprentice, not very old in the business. Their harness was like that of the second pair and their spreader was attached to the sixth chain.

*In 1876, L. F. Allen, speaking about American draught horses, says: "Of this class * * * first in order stands the Conestoga of Pennsylvania. * * * Nearly or quite a hundred years ago, when the settlements of that state had extended westward over the Allegheny Mountains, when towns began to spring up, and heavy transportation between them and the seaboard became necessary, the huge

*Pennsylvania Report of Agriculture, 1877.

canvas-covered wagons, carrying six tons and upwards of merchandise, were drawn by spans of four to eight horses, with sometimes a ninth one in single harness as a leader.   Those horses ranged from sixteen and one-half to seventeen and one-half hands high, with bodies solid and bulky in proportion.   Caravans of those teams were seen at all seasons with bearskin housings upon the hames and an arch of bells above them, with the driver seated on the near wheel horse, and a more picturesque spectacle of the kind can hardly be imagined. Their usual rate of travel was about twelve or fourteeen miles a day. * * *   It is doubtful if a better class of heavy draught horses than they ever existed.   It is claimed by some that the Conestoga has been bred to this high degree of excellence by crosses with the thoroughbred English horse.''

Supposing that this horse did come to Lancaster County from the English settlements about Philadelphia, he could claim a long and honorable lineage and boast of having come over with William the Conquerer, for the English draught horses or black cart horses were descended from those great black horses of France, who came across the channel cased in armor and carrying on their broad backs a husky, armor-clad knight.

Many Conestogas were black, but mixed breeding soon produced bays (probably from the Suffolk Punch), and later, dappled greys.

In The Practical Farmer (Cincinnati, 1842), Edward Hooper says that "the best model of the heavier kind of farmer's or wagoner's horse is the Suffolk Punch.   It strongly resembles the famous Chester Balls and the Conestoga horses of Pennsylvania.   * * * * Its color is almost invariably bright chestnut;   * * * *   all the heavy English draught horses have of late been crossed by the French or Flanders breed with evident improvement.''

The Honorable John Strohm, of New Providence, Pennsylvania, writing about "The Conestoga Horse" in the United States Department of Agriculture Report for 1863, says: "I am fully impressed with the belief that the superior excellence attributed to the Conestoga horse is not derived from any strain or breed that can now be traced to its origin, as Chester County and the vicinity of Philadelphia were partially settled and considerably improved before any settlement was effected in the Conestoga Valley, it is quite probable that the first immigrants to this valley derived their first stock of horses from their nearest neighbors, inhabiting the named localities; and it requires no great stretch of the imagination to suppose that the first settlers in Pennsylvania who came here with William Penn, or some of their immediate successors, brought some of those useful animals with them from England, from which the whole stock of horses in the country at that time was derived. Being well fed, comfortably stabled and never overworked or abused, this horse attained the full development of his natural powers, seldom found in any other country, and much surpassing the original stock. The deep interest with which the farmers of this region regarded this noble animal naturally stimulated a desire to improve the stock * * * * their aim being to produce a strong, well set and tolerably active animal with great powers of endurance. Emigration into the western country soon necessitated the hauling of supplies from Philadelphia to Pittsburgh, seldom farther, for there they were put on rafts or keel boats. The usual route was through Lancaster, Columbia or Mari-

Conestoga Wagon Harness, the "Fair of the Iron Horse," 1927. Photograph by courtesy of The U. S. National Museum.

etta, over the Alleghenies to the Forks of the Ohio or to Lake Erie. This was before the construction of turnpikes and canals, and the capacious wagons which the Conestoga farmers then had, with their heavy teams of large, fat, sleek horses, were the best means of transportation which the times and circumstances of the country then afforded. These wagons and teams attracted attention and commanded admiration wherever they appeared. The farmers of those days seemed fully to appreciate the importance of their teams and evinced considerable taste and no little pride in their style of fitting them out. In the harness and trimmings of their teams they frequently indulged in expense that approached extravagance. In addition to what was indispensable, articles by some deemed mere decoration were sometimes appended and served to increase the admiration which the noble animals, to which they were attached, so universally attracted.   It was, indeed, an animating sight to see five or six highly fed horses, half covered with heavy bear skins, or decorated with gaudily fringed housings, surmounted with a set of finely-toned bells, their bridles adorned with loops of red trimming, moving over the ground with a brisk, elastic step, snorting disdainfully at surrounding objects, as if half conscious of their superior appearance and participating in the pride that swelled the bosom of their master and driver."

This was apparently before 1790.   Then followed the first turnpikes and the full development of Conestoga wagon transportation, until the railroads and canals began to take away the business after 1830, and western horses and mules began to take their places in the Pennsylvania farmer's teams.   The Conestoga pageant, with its picturesque characters and its resounding activity, passed on, one step in progress finished, and making way for the next.

W. J. Kennedy, of the Iowa Agricultural College, writing on "Selecting and Judging Horses" in the year book of the United States Department of Agriculture for 1902, says: "The Conestoga horse had no growth of long hair or feather between the knee and fetlock, as this would have been an unending source of trouble to the driver on muddy roads; a long tail also was a nuisance.   The feet were moderately large but not flat, the top of the neck or crest well arched, body and legs rather short than long, stride rather long than short, temperament rather docile than nervous, movement forward steady, and not wabbling, height to withers sixteen to seventeen hands, and weight 1,800 pounds or over in normal condition.   The horse must be well muscled, less so than a brewery wagon horse; and the best colors in order are found to be bay, black, grey, brown, chestnut, sorrel, roan, with not too much marking.   Although strong, these heavy horses need careful attention to keep them in health and the horse doctor is needed occasionally.   The mule was later found to need practically no doctoring, lived long, worked hard, and was tractable when well treated, so that he found a permanent place in farm work.   Hardy western horses were low priced and did not eat so much as the Conestogas, and were found to be strong enough for farm work.   So that, when wagoning stopped, Othello's occupation was gone, and the Conestoga breed of horses became a memory."

From the Wagoner of the Alleghenies, by T. Buchanan Read

CHAPTER X

Of Sundry Conestoga Wagons and Wagoners

MR. NEVIN W. MOYER, of Linglestown, has the old tar bucket and jack dated 1791, which belonged to his gallant ancestor. Daniel Moyer brought a piano to his home in his Conestoga wagon, which is said to have been the first piano in all Berks County. When his son, Daniel junior, born in 1797, was old enough, his father also imported in the same Conestoga a music master to teach his son to play on the violin. Small Daniel knew the sound of his father's bells, and hid behind the wood pile on music lesson days. He must have been found, however, for in 1825 when La Fayette was escorted through Harrisburg with much pomp, and many white-topped wagons in the cavalcade, young Daniel Moyer was the bugler of the Dauphin County cavalry. He was for many years a wagoner.

John Whitesides opened a tavern near to the market house on West King Street, Lancaster, in 1812, at the sign of "The Lion." From the collection of Miss Dorothy Flinn, Bleak House, Kinzers, Pennsylvania.

The Sign of the Grape Tavern, North Queen Street, Lancaster, Pennsylvania.

The Grape Tavern was opened in 1741. The large wooden bunch of grapes was made for Adam Reigart, who kept it during Revolutionary days, when several committee meetings of the Continental Congress were held there.

In 1804 John Michael became the tavern keeper and called his house "The Conestoga Waggon." Later, under John Michael's son, it was again called "The Grape Tavern."

The original is in the collection of Miss Dorothy Flinn, Bleak House, Kinzers, Pennsylvania.

In 1811 on the roads to the west, in the mountain fastnesses, lurked one Lewis, a robber; he would station himself with his men at the top of a long steep hill and waylay teams as they struggled over, one at a time. Daniel Moyer once encountered him. For every one of the thousands of wagons that were driven through the great state of Pennsylvania, there must have been similar little homely stories and tales of adventure of those far days.

The Green Tree Inn of Chester County, one of the many on the King's Highway, was kept by Henry Coffmann. Each night his tavern yard was filled with teams and his bar room with wagoners. Sergeant Andrew Wallace was a permanent guest here, and entertainer. He lived to be a hundred and four years old, and had served in the French and Indian War under both Braddock and Forbes. He had also fought in the Revolution in the Fourth Pennsylvania Regulars, commanded by Colonel Anthony Wayne. At the Brandywine it was Sergeant Wallace who carried

General LaFayette, wounded, from the field,　He had also fought at Three Rivers, Paoli, Valley Forge, Monmouth, Stony Point, and Yorktown, so he had many stories to tell, and he never lacked an audience.

In 1800 John Eichelberger opened a tavern in York on West Market Street, called the York County Wagon.　Upon his signpost there swung a painting of a big Conestoga Wagon with six-horse team and bells.

In the Cumberland Valley there was greater distance between the taverns than on the Philadelphia - Lancaster Road, but the wagoner could help himself to apples from the orchards along the way.

Sometimes there were two roads, either of which might be taken, on the poorer of which you saved toll. This was true between Shippensburg and Chambersburg, where, besides the turnpike, there was a shorter road through Strasburgh.

The Globe Tavern, York, Pennsylvania, where General LaFayette stopped in 1824, from a contemporary print. Courtesy of Miss Margaretta Wagner.

In 1800 John Eichelberger kept a tavern in York on West Market Street, called the York County Waggon, whose sign showed a picture of a Conestoga Wagon.

At one time there was talk of wide-tired wagons being allowed to go toll free, on the supposition that they rolled the roads rather than wore them.　An ingenious wagoner is said to have built his wagon with this idea in mind, with tires eight inches wide and the rear axle narrower than the front one, so that the wheels actually rolled three feet of road as he traveled.　His idea was not successful, however, and his wagon never came back from Philadelphia.

If, instead of taking the road through Lancaster and Columbia, the wagoner turned off of the King's Highway at Downing's Town, and took the road to Topton, there was Harris' Ferry to be crossed. Farrar's Ferry, three miles below, was cheaper and many wagons crossed there.　In the Winter time, when sleighs and pedestrians

TO FARMERS & WAGONERS.

Feeling desirous that you should receive the benefit of a WAGON RETARDER, which I have constructed and now have in use, you are at liberty to have it applied to your Wagons without incurring an expense more than the original; as I do not intend to patent it. This machine is of simple construction, costs but little when compared to the many and important advantages resulting; it acts very powerfully upon the wheels when descending hills, in so much, that one horse is able to stop a Wagon heavy laden without the least difficulty, which must of necessity prevent the many and dangerous accidents to which horses and drivers are subject: It will therefore be much to your interest to send your wagons to my blacksmith's shop and have them fixed, or those living at a distance who cannot make it convenient to send their wagons, may obtain (by addressing a line to me, post paid) all the necessary information respecting it. I have also the running gears of a new broad wheel wagon well ironed for sale, which will be sold on moderate terms.

WILLIAM SCHNEBLY.

Hagers-town, Washington county, } 6-5w.
State of Maryland, Dec. 7.   }

To Farmers, Millers and Distillers.

THE subscriber continues to hold that large and commodious Ware-House, situated near the mouth of Conococheague creek,—where he will store Flour, Whiskey, &c. He is also provided with Boats to carry produce to Washington City or Georgetown, on terms suitable to the times ; and will be responsible for accidents that may occur in carriage.

He will deliver Flour in Baltimore much lower than wagon carriage ; it would be advisable for millers to turn their attention to that route, as wagons become scarce in the spring and summer seasons.

JOSEPH HOLLMAN.

Williams-Port, Feb. 7.   15—tf.

N. B. He has on hand several hundred bushels of

Stone Coal,

which will be sold low, for Cash.

Flour, Whiskey, &c. &c.

G. B. WILSON begs leave to inform his friends & customers, that he has purchased all the Stock and interest of Mr. Orndorff, in the late firm of Orndorff & Wilson ; and having associated with him, his Brother Mr. CHARLES WILSON, the

FLOUR & PRODUCE BUSINESS will in future be conducted by them, at the *Old Stand. No. 243, Market-St.* under the firm of G. B. WILSON & CO.

Who offer for Sale, on pleasing terms,

300 tons PLASTER PARIS,

2000 bush. Ground Allum SALT,

250 sacks Liverpool fill'd Fine do.

15000 lbs. Green Jamaica COFFEE,

MAKAREL, SHAD, HERRINGS,

TAR, OIL, &c.

Together with an assort'nt of the best *Brands*

OLD 4TH PROOF WHISKEY,

Viz :—Miller's, Welty's, Shees's, Zeigler's, Washabaugh's, &c. &c.

G. B. WILSON & CO. will at all times purchase good wagon PORK, or they will receive it FOR SALE on commission. They will also receive GOODS directed to their care, and forward them by careful wagoners without delay—Merchants will find it to their advantage to direct to their   Ob't. Serv'ts,

G. B. WILSON & CO.
13—4w.

☞ Orders will be strictly attended to.
Baltimore, January 25.

crossed on the ice, a channel was cut for the Conestoga ferry.   In the mountains, taverns were plentiful.

It is a dizzy thought, the idea of those great Conestogas, with their heavy loads and teams, going over the five high ridges between Philadelphia and Pittsburgh, and making their way up and down those grades, even as we know them today, at McConnellsville and Stoyestown.   Very often a pedestrian was met who was glad to attend the brake in exchange for a ride upon the lazy board. Many subsequently successful men made their entrance into Pittsburgh as brake tenders.   Lacking this assistance, the wagoner tended his own brake, fastening the lever down by hooking one of the links of its chain over the pin on the brake beam. The professional wagoner seems to have worn a wide-brimmed hat, a homespun suit and high top boots, called stogies, and a beard, the sign of manhood. He had a great coat in winter, and home-knit mittens and scarf.

Wagoner's stable at the Clay Hotel on the old Downington-Harrisburg Road. "About 1833, Mr. Erb erected a barn and what is now known as the Old Shed to the west of his hotel.   As this hotel was situated on the old Paxtang Road, it was a great stopping place for the Conestoga wagons and many a thrilling adventure took place there.   The Paxtang Road did not run then as the Harrisburg-Downington turnpike now runs, but passed between the hotel and the Old Shed through the orchard to Laubers Corner.   The custom in those days was for the horses to sleep close to the wagon, and the men on the floor.   When the Pike or Horseshoe Pike, as it was then called, was built, this hotel continued as a stopping place for the Conestoga wagons and Irish drovers."—Proceedings of the Lancaster County Historical Society, Vol. 20, No. 3.

"During this period it was called the Red Lion Hotel, and had a sign with a red lion on it, but the name was changed in 1868 to the Eagle Hotel, and it is now called the Clay Hotel." H. K. Landis.

He carried no weapons, except perhaps brass knuckles and a black jack, for a fight was forever looming on the horizon, especially on the western road.   There were many things to quarrel about, and the wagoner in the popular mind became a dashing daredevil, who was to the Pennsylvania countryside what the cowboy was, later, to the west.   Thomas Buchanan Read, in "The Wild Wagoner," writes —

> "While bold as an embodied storm,
> Strode in a dark and stalwart form
> As the startled keeper welcomed in
> The feared and famous wagoner.

Captain John Simpson and his family, of Montgomery County, in 1818, made the journey of four hundred and fifty miles to the Ohio by wagon. It took them five weeks and three days. All of the time they cooked by camp fires and slept in the white-topped Conestoga. They followed the Lancaster Road to Columbia, where they crossed the bridge and journeyed to Chambersburg, through the Cumberland Valley to Bedford, through Somerset County, in the grassy glades of the Alleghenies to Brownsville, and from there on the National Road to Wheeling.

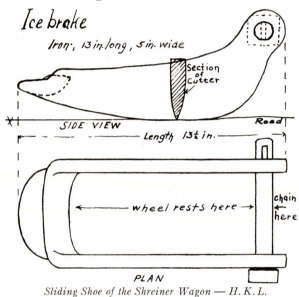

Ice brake

Iron: 13 in. long, 5 in. wide

Section of Cutter

SIDE VIEW   Road

Length 13¾ in.

wheel rests here →   chain here

PLAN

Sliding Shoe of the Shreiner Wagon — H. K. L.

At the time of year when farmers were not busy on their farms, they often carried freight in their wagons, and they were called by the regular wagoners, militia or sharp-shooters. The farmer carried feed for his horses as well as food for himself, while the regular depended on the inns. Often the farmer had extra wheels for his wagon, using small ones on the farm and large ones for road work. Sometimes there were only two large extra wheels, and these were used as the back wheels of the road wagon, and the back wheels of the farm wagon became the front wheels of the wagon on the road.

Many a teamster started as a boy driving his father's team. Wagoning was a young man's profession. When he married he left the road and went back to the farm.

On arriving at the tavern after a day's journey, the wagon was left in the wagon yard and the horses were watered and ranged, three on each side of the feed box, which was placed on the wagon tongue. The wagoner often slept out of doors with his team on fine Summer nights. In the Winter time the wagon was driven upon planks, so

*A Continental Note for eight Spanish milled dollars,
issued at Philadelphia in 1775.
Courtesy of Mr. C. H. Martin*

that the wheels would not freeze to the ground during the night. Then the wagoner took his mattress, which was about two feet wide and four inches thick and which he carried in a roll in the back of the wagon, and taking it in, threw it on the bar-room floor, where he chose to sleep, before the fire, and woe betide the person who changed it.

At McGowan's tavern, there was a fifteen-foot fireplace, and at Captain Statler's tavern the fireplace was twelve feet wide, and a horse hauled in the great logs through a special door.

At the corner of the bar room was a short bar, where whiskey in clear glass bottles, carefully labeled Old Rye or Monongahela, might be had from mine host or the bar maid for three cents a glass.

The cost of a night's lodging, feed for six horses, meals for the teamster, and three drinks of whiskey, one before supper, a night cap, and one before breakfast, was about seventy-five cents.

After supper there were stories and singing, and sometimes there were neighboring spelling bees or singing schools, fairs or dances to go to.

Precedence is said to have come with age. The

*The Spanish milled dollar, or Pillar (of Hercules) dollar,
which was the money standard of colonial America. Their
value is eight reals and they were the familiar "pieces of
eight" of pirate stories.
The one real piece or levy, and the half real or fip, bore
the same designs but were smaller coins. The two real piece
was also similar, and about the size of a present-day
quarter. It was called a shilling.
Courtesy of Mr. C. H. Martin*

oldest wagoner first made his choice of a place to sleep and was also the first to leave the inn the next morning.   At early dawn they fed their horses, ate their own hearty breakfasts and were off with a rumbling of wheels and a cracking of whips.   Often in the Winter time the wagoners had to shovel snow as they traveled.

Local Paper Currency of Conestoga days.
Courtesy of Mr. C. H. Martin

Many a farmer drove his own team, and many freight wagons were owned by responsible shippers and manufacturers.   An advertisement in the Philadelphia paper in 1818 reads:

"Thomas N. Souders, having opened a store at No. 312 Market Street for the reception of merchandise to be transported to the Western Country in Waggons, offers his services to the merchants generally, to take charge of their goods to be forwarded to Pittsburgh or any part of the western country.   He flatters himself that, by his attention and the experience he has acquired, he will be enabled to give general satisfaction."

In the Lancaster Journal of May 12, 1817, the following advertisement appears:

"Western Hotel.

Sign of the Wagon.

The subscriber informs his friends and the public generally, that he continues to keep a house of public entertainment in Orange Street, corner of Water Street, in the borough of Lancaster, where travelers or boarders may be conveniently accommodated, either by the week or day.   Being provided with a spacious yard and sufficiency of stabling, sheds for horses and wagons, also with all kinds of horse food, waggoners will find it an advantageous and convenient place to stop at. He flatters himself, by a strict attention to his business, and by always keeping the best liquors, to merit a share of the public patronage.

John Landis."

These were busy and prosperous times on the Philadelphia and Lancaster turnpike, and the Conestoga trail that led to the west. There were said to be three thousand regulars between Philadelphia and Pittsburgh daily.

Local Paper Currency of Conestoga days
Courtesy of Mr. C. H. Martin

At first each consignor had paid a fractional part of the cost of the load, but later there was a regular charge per hundred weight.

About 1880 an old Pittsburgh merchant wrote the president of the Pennsylvania Railroad, "Before any canal was made, I shipped 800 barrels of flour one winter from Pittsburgh to Philadelphia by wagon, the freight on which was $2,400, or $3 per barrel. That was called 'back loading' by Conestoga wagon, six horses and bells. My first load of goods sixty years ago, from Philadelphia to Pittsburgh, cost four dollars per hundred pounds."

Mordecai Hayes, wagoner of Embreeville, Chester County, has left an account book showing the charges for the hauling of various loads "coffe and reasons, malt, hogsheads of molasses, shugar, hogsheads of rum, sope, cags of nails, stone, coal;" the most interesting entry occurs in the year 1827, and reads, "To hauling ten thousand cents for the Bank C. C., 75 cents." These were probably the big copper pennies which he brought out from Philadelphia to the bank of Chester County in West Chester. It doubtless took his fine six-

American Pewter Dollar of Continental Times.
Courtesy of Mr. C. H. Martin

horse team a whole day to go, and another to return, over the rough roads.

Although after 1793 there was money of American coinage, the big copper cent, the quarter, the half dollar and the dollar, it was not until after 1830 that we were able to mint money fast enough to supply our needs and to finally displace the foreign coins in common use. After the revolution French crowns became common, and the Spanish-American dollar was the standard and unit of the money of the republic. The first silver dollar coined by the United States mint in 1785 was patterned after it and was of the same value. The border of this Spanish, eight real dollar, was milled, and not the edge, so it was called the milled dollar. These Spanish dollars are the pieces of eight of pirate fame. There were eight reals in a piece, or a dollar. The one real piece, one-eighth of a dollar, the eleven-penny bit, was the famous "levy," and the half real, worth five pence in English coin, was the fippenny bit or "fip," and was sometimes called a picayune, from its name in Louisiana. With pieces of eight, levys and fips in his pocket, the wagoner was sure of a welcome anywhere.

The pioneers of America exchanged their products through barter and were fortunate to secure coin of any kind. However, many of them had

Local Paper Currency of Conestoga Days
Courtesy of Mr. C. H. Martin

During the Civil War, this medal, struck by
S. H. Zahm in 1861, passed as one cent.
Courtesy of Mr. C. H. Martin

brought with them coins of their native lands, and these were gladly accepted in exchange; English money was the most common of all, though England preferred getting raw material from us in exchange for our purchases from them. Massachusetts had issued its first paper money in 1690; Connecticut and New York in 1709; Pennsylvania in 1723 and New Jersey in 1724.

Exchange in 1702 was against us by one-third above par. This discrimination only served to stimulate the spread of foreign coin through the colonies, so that in 1800 the English pound in Pennsylvania was worth only two dollars and sixty-seven cents in Spanish silver dollars, as compared with the present exchange of about four dollars and eighty-six cents. The value of English money, reckoned by the generally accepted standard of the Spanish milled dollar (the peso, pillar dollar, piece of eight, originally coined for Spanish America in 8, 4, 1 and one-half real pieces), varied throughout the states. While England in 1807 valued the English pound at $4.44, New England quoted $3.32; New York and North Carolina $2.50; New Jersey, Pennsylvania and Maryland $2.67; Virginia $3.32; and Georgia $4.24.

In a New England almanac of 1797, a list of current coins is given. English and French crowns are worth $1.10; a pistareen, twenty cents;

Local paper currency in use during the Civil War.
Courtesy of Mr. C. H. Martin

nine pence (so called, but in fact a Spanish real, or one-eighth of a Spanish dollar) twelve and a half cents. The half pistareen is ten cents and the half real six and a quarter cents. The quarter pistareen or half dime is the five-cent piece.

In his "Progress of America," John MacGregor enumerated some foreign coins brought in through commerce — the guinea, the joe, the half joe, the doubloon and pistole in gold; the dollar, the pistareen, and the British shilling and sixpence in silver. In almanacs of 1800

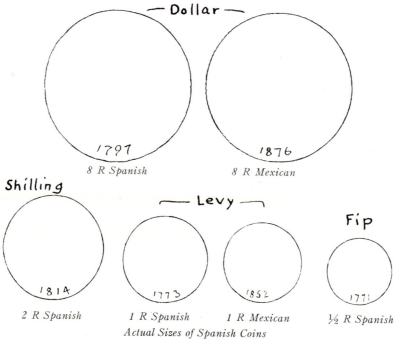

Actual Sizes of Spanish Coins

we find quoted a Portuguese Moidore and Johannes, Spanish doubloons, the Caroline and German ducats, Dutch guilders (gulden or florins) of two stivers each, and Swedish coin.

Wagoners, teaming from one part of the country to another, had to make provision for the difference in the exchange values of the coined money. To complicate the condition further, there were local issues of coins having no fixed value, and numerous issues of paper money, in which there was small confidence outside of the locality where they were well known. In Massachusetts in 1750, a shilling in coin was worth eleven shillings in paper. The Revolutionary War added Continental paper money to the colonial issues and, until these were all redeemed, there was much suspicion of any unfamiliar money.

Popular coins were given popular names. The Spanish milled dollar was called the pillar dollar when it bore the Spanish coat of arms, and the Mexican dollar when it showed a liberty cap on a sunburst. The half dollar was not common, but the quarter dollar was named a shilling. After the Revolution paper currency was issued by banks in large quantities, and most of them failed. There were also private issues by merchants and other business people, but in spite of the instability of the currency trade flourished and the big Conestogas hauled more and more merchandise. Banks continued to issue their own notes, and so did various firms and corporations, whose paper money at the time of the Civil War was known as "wild cat" and "shin plasters" because of its very dubious worth.

Sometimes the owner of a team bought a load of merchandise at Philadelphia or Baltimore, which he hauled to Pittsburgh and sold. The money he received for it had to be such as would be accepted in the east for more goods. It was impossible for buyers of western horses and cattle to carry enough coin for their purchases, so they hid paper money on their persons, which they exchanged for coin in Ohio and Kentucky, so that they could pay the western farmers.

Often a prosperous teamster would own several Conestoga wagons, and driving the leading and handsomest one himself, would start off his proud procession. Usually the horses were matched, all blacks, or bays, or grays; they moved along with proudly arched necks, conscious of their importance and the distinction and pomp of the pageant. Sometimes twenty to a hundred wagons would follow one another in a row, and at one time there were said to be ten thousand around Philadelphia. An American poet has written —

> "The old road blossoms with romance
> Of covered vehicles of every grade,
> From ox cart of most primitive design
> To Conestoga wagons with their fine
> Deep dusted, six-horse teams in heavy gear,
> High hames and chiming bells — to childish ear
> And eye entrancing as the glittering train
> Of some sun-smitten pageant of old Spain."

Wild animals became a nuisance along the Conestoga trail, and in an old Bedford paper is this regretable account. "On Friday, December fourth, 1818, about 700 men from neighboring townships formed a hunting party. The signal was first given on French Town Mountain and the circle of forty miles of horn blowing to horn was completed in fifteen minutes. The hunters progressed to a center in Nysox Township, used guns as long as they could with safety, then bayonets and clubs, poles, pitchforks, etc. 5 bears, 9 wolves and 14 foxes were killed and 300 deer. It was estimated that more than double that number escaped. The excursion closed with great mirth at a tavern."

It isn't unusual to see some of the descendants of the escaping two-thirds. If you are fortunate you may catch a glimpse of a shadow dappled deer peering daintily at the strange creatures which sweep over the hills of the Conestoga trail today.

The old tavern and bridge at the Juniata Crossings. The Juniata was the largest stream to be crossed on the journey west. At first there was a primitive ferry. Later a "chain bridge" was built, a little below the present covered one. Large chains spanned the river and were anchored to a stone pier on one side and to the rocks on the other, where deep wheel marks can still be seen. In 1814 the covered bridge was started, which is still in use. The eastern end was destroyed by ice and floods in 1885 and was rebuilt, but the rest is the original structure with its great hand-hewn timbers.

There was a tavern at the Juniata Crossings in 1795. The present one was built in 1818 by Hugh Dennison, out of native stone. During the forties, when stage and wagon travel was at its height, the tavern was kept by George McGraw.

The old inns are there, too, the one at Schellsburg, one at the Juniata, and others but sadly modernized on the outside, at least. The one exception is the old log house just outside of Bedford by the mill stream, with its great log fire in the tap room, with its cranes and pots; its doors with hand-wrought hinges, and its candle light and old mahogany. And just beyond is the old covered bridge over the Juniata, and the crossing below, where the rocks still show the heavy wheel marks of Conestoga days.

"Travel in 1830" from a painting by Mr. Stanley M. Arthurs. Courtesy of the Artist.

CHAPTER XI

Of the Heyday of Wagoning

WAGONING was at its zenith around 1830. T. B. Searight, in "The Old Pike," says that the line teams, which were run by a company, changed their horses every fifteen miles; and that the Conestoga trail to the West looked more like an avenue leading into a great city than a rural road. There were numberless coaches, great fleets of six-horse Conestogas, and caravans of horses and sheep and cattle. There were stage houses every twelve miles and wagon stands at every mile.

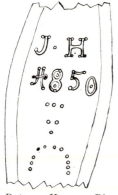

Date on Hammer-Pin Hasp. Drawing from original. See page 117.

Part of the driver's work was to grease the wagon axles. This had to be done often. The wheel was raised with the jack, the linch pin was removed and the grease was put on with a paddle. If the wagon was loaded and couldn't be jacked up, a feather was used by the wagoner, who applied the grease between the hub and the axle and tickled away the squeaks.

The stopper hole in the hub mounting was wedged shut with a corncob, so that a sudden jolt could not bounce the linch pin out of place. The careful teamster kept a good supply of corncobs with him always.

Wagoners who did not own their own teams earned from eight to ten dollars a month, and sometimes made a little on the side by buying some merchandise at one end and selling it at the other of their journey.

Joseph Ritner, the "Wagon Boy of the Alleghenies," was a wagoner who became Governor of Pennsylvania. All loyal wagoners, on seeing supporters of the opposing candidate, an Irishman, would sing:

> "Wote nunner der Irisher,
> der Joseph Ritner is der mon,
> der unser Staat regenen Kon."*

*(Vote down the Irishman; Joseph Ritner is the man that can govern our state.)

To a small boy a journey by wagon was a great event to be eagerly prepared for, and to be thought about and boasted of for many weeks thereafter. From Springfield Township in Bucks County, from five to twelve wagons would prepare to go in together to the market at Philadelphia, forty-two miles away, with their pork and poultry, butter and eggs and flax. In 1834 the roads were still very poor. The horses were fed and pampered for days before, to prepare them for the fatigues of the journey. And little boys, fortunate enough to be taken along, took with them hog bristles that they could sell to brush makers, or rabbits, or partridges, or chestnuts, shellbarks or walnuts, for which they might buy a knife or a harmonica, a cap or a book or some candy.

A farm wagon, built in 1824 for the Davis family, is to be seen at the Berks County Historical Society, with many other reminders of Conestoga days. This was used for hauling produce and town necessities to and from Reading.

The National Road was another road to the West, ending at Wheeling. It had been proposed in 1797 and was finished in 1818 by the National Government, and many a great Conestoga rumbled over its continuous

Western Hotel.

CHRISTOPHER BRENNER respectfully informs his friends and the public, that he has taken and commenced keeping that well known Public House in the city of Lancaster,

Corner of Orange & Water Streets,

Lately occupied by Nathan C Scofield, sign of the WESTERN HOTEL, where he is prepared with the best of Liquors, Provisions, &c. necessary to entertain those who may honor him with a visit.

This establishment is perhaps better calculated for the accommodation of drovers, waggoners and travellers, than any other in this city. In addition to the many advantages which it already possesses, the Stabling will be enlarged and repaired in the best manner, to suit that portion of patronage which he is desirous of accommodating.

C. B. Pledges himself that nothing shall be wanting on his part, to render general satisfaction.

REMOVAL.

GEORGE MORRY

INFORMS his friends and the public, that he has removed to the public house lately kept by JOHN RUPLEY, in West King Street, in the city of Lancaster, sign of the Wagon—where he is provided with good Liquors, Provisions, and other necessaries for the accommodation of those who may favour him with a call.

The house is large and convenient, his Stabling is good; and, in short, if any thing can be effected by industry, and attention to business, he flatters himself with the hope of a liberal share of the public patronage

apr 18   7-3nq

Advertisements of Wagoner's Inns, in the Lancaster Intelligencer of December 19, 1828 hills into the green and fertile valleys of Kentucky and Ohio. It was a fine turnpike sixty feet wide, of three-inch broken stone, covered with gravel and rolled. The work was done by "that great contractor Mordecai Cochran, with his immortal Irish brigade a thousand strong, with their carts, wheelbarrows, picks, shovels, and blasting tools, who graded the commons and climbed the mountain side, leaving behind them a roadway good enough for an emperor."

Conestoga Wagon, from a painting in the Pennsylvania Historical Society, by F. O. C. Darley, 1874

A quaint and pastoral glimpse of wagoning is to be found in a note from Mrs. Frank B. Black, of Somerset. She writes: "My own people were engaged in this old business, driving wagons between Mt. Pleasant, Westmoreland County, Pennsylvania, and Baltimore. The wagons were only a part of this primitive railway. Attendant were the cattle, horses and even turkeys, that went on foot with the caravan. People, too, often moved from place to place under the protection of the wagons, paying for the privilege by helping with the stock and guarding the cargoes." Mr. T. J. Phillips, of Atglen, Chester County, remembers a big slave, Black Nat, who drove a team for Mr. Phillip's grandfather. Black Nat, besides being a driver, was a great trader and invariably came back with better horses than he started with.

The levee at Pittsburgh was crowded in these days with bales of cotton, barrels of whiskey and flour, bags of grain and pig iron. Besides the hauling cost there were other charges for labor, storage, insurance, cartage, rattage, and commissions, all considered legitimate. Once a large load of pig iron was shipped and all of the usual charges were rendered, including "rattage." The irate consignor wrote that in the future he would send his iron to some other shipping point, where the rats had not as remarkable digestive powers as those at Pittsburgh.

By far the greatest number of stories of the old wagon deal with the later days on the road to the West. Of all of these, none is more vivid and delightful than that written by David Eby. As a little boy eight years old, in 1832, when his father kept the Stoufferstown Tavern, he remembered seeing the German emi-

---

...house of Major Frederick Hambright, *This Afternoon*, the 25th instant, at 2 o'clock—to which all who wish to become members are invited to attend.
dec 25

CITY GUARDS.

THE Corps will assemble in parade order at the Court House, on *Thursday next*, the 1st of January, at 9 o'clock, A. M. for the purpose of escorting the Union Troop into the City. By order of the Capt
JNO. A. MESSENKOP, O. S.
dec 26

PENNSYLVANIA RAIL-WAY.

PROPOSALS will be received at the Office of the Pennsylvania Railway, in the City of Lancaster, until 4 o'clock on the 27th day of January next, for the grading and road formation of a portion of the said Railway, beginning at the borough of Columbia, and extending eastward 20 miles;—and also for the grading and road formation of another portion of the said Railway, beginning at a point near the residence of the late Judge Peters, on the Schuylkill river, and extending westward a distance of 20 miles.

Proposals will also be received at the same time for the necessary bridges and culverts on the portions described. The line will be distinctly marked and divided into sections of conveniet size. Contractors, on application to the Engineer or either of his Assistants, will be furnished with a list of the sections, containing accurate descriptions of the several kinds of work embraced within them. Printed forms for proposals will also be furnished, and no bid will be noticed unless made in such form.

By order of the Canal Commissioners.
JOS. M'ILVAINE, *Sec'y.*
dec 26   44-td

Drawing Materials, PERFUMERY.

For Sale at the Drug Store of the Subscriber. Water Colors in boxes, and by

From the Lancaster Intelligencer, December 26, 1828
See page 120.

grants going west over the turnpike, from Baltimore to Pittsburgh. They traveled in Conestoga wagon trains. Their clothing, their bedding and cooking utensils, were carried in the wagons, and sometimes the women and children rode in them, while the men and boys walked. At night the women slept in the wagon and the men were given quarters in the barn. The cooking was done along the wayside

Studebaker Shop and Home, Ashland, Ohio, 1835.
Courtesy of The Studebaker Corporation. See page 117.

in gypsy fashion, and the provisions were gathered during the day as they traveled along. Most of the home seekers passed during the summer.

John Miller, a well-known wagoner of the day, owned several fine six-horse Conestoga teams and was a great favorite with the emigrants. As he wagoned along, with his precious freight and oddly-dressed escort afoot, he exchanged sallies of wit with passing wagoners, all in a jolly humor. At the inn at night, when the wagoners gave an account of their day's journey and the whereabouts of others on the road, as was the custom, a hearty laugh was sure to follow the final announcement, "And oh, yes, John Miller is coming from Baltimore with another load of Dutch for Pittsburgh." In those days the turnpike was lined with teams and all inns did a thriving business.

In 1849 Mr. Eby became a wagoner, his first trip being to Pittsburgh with two other regulars. Upon the completion of the Penn-

Two views of a wagon built by John Studebaker, blacksmith and wagonmaker, who lived near Gettysburg, in 1830. In this wagon he took his wife and six children, while two other wagons carried his household goods, anvil and tools to the new home which he built in the western country at Ashland, Ohio. This is of the prairie-schooner type. Courtesy of The Studebaker Corporation. See page 118.

sylvania Railroad four years later, the long trips were abandoned, but he still did piece loading, which meant taking freight from the ends of the railroad lines to towns not reached by the trains. He speaks of the hazards of the mountain roads, of the great, flat, smooth rocks on Laurel Hill, where many a horse has slipped and fallen. He says that from Chambersburg to Pittsburgh, in 1853, there was a tavern for every mile of road, just as there had been on the old Lancaster Pike sixty years earlier.

He remembers when the troops marched along the road on their way to

Mexico in 1846, while their baggage was carried in the great white-topped Conestoga wagons.

"Many a fleet of them,
In one long, upward winding
  row.
It ever was a noble sight,
As from the distant mountain
  height,
Or quiet valley far below,
Their snow-white covers
  looked like sail."

Conestoga Wagon, of the farm type, c. 1850, showing feed box, tool box, side boards, hoops, etc. Lancaster County. Landis Valley Museum.

The wagoners were a noisy, jolly crew, who loved to frolic and dance. At the end of the day, when the horses stood eating contentedly under the stars, and their bells were silent, the music of a violin was usually heard inside the tavern, and the wagoners, who had walked probably the greater part of the twenty miles that their teams had traveled that day, danced whatever tune the fiddle sang; the Virginia Reel, the French Reel, Four Square, Jim Crow, or Hoe

A dappled gray six-horse team belonging to Armour and Company. One of these teams, during a whole summer, followed the Barnum and Bailey Circus, appearing at the end of every circus parade.

The fine six-horse team of Wilson and Company, who still maintain a team of this kind. The horses are kept in splendid condition and are shown not only at county fairs throughout the country in the Fall, but at other horse shows.

Down, and for refreshments there was "Monongahela" at three cents a glass.

Mr. Eby was the wagoner who hauled part of the ammunition and arms for John Brown's party to Williamsport, where it was shipped

A modern Pennsylvania farm wagon and eight-mule team, which has superceded the old Conestoga. (January 7, 1929.) Courtesy of H. C. Frey.

George Washington writes in his diary, "Thursday, 16th (November, 1786), on my return home, found Mons. Campoint, sent by the Marqs. de la Fayette, with the Jack and two she Asses, which he had procured for me in the island of Malta, and which had arrived at Baltimore with the Chinese Pheasants, &c., had with my Overseer &c, got there before me." (The jacks and jennets were sent in furtherance of Washington's desire to introduce a good breed of mules in the United States. The King of Spain sent him a pair, one of which died on the way.) "The Spanish jack seems calculated to breed for heavy, slow draught; and the others (the la Fayette jacks), for the saddle or lighter carriages. From these altogether I hope to secure a race of extraordinary goodness, which will stock the country. Their longevity and cheap keeping will be circumstances much in their favor. I am convinced, from the little experiments I have made with the ordinary mules (which perform as much labor, with vastly less feeding, than horses), that those of a superior quality will be the best cattle we can employ for the harness; and, indeed, in a few years, I intend to drive no other in my carriage, having appropriated for the sole purpose of breeding them, upwards of twenty of my best mares."— (G. W. to Arthur Young, December 4, 1788.)

An amusing sketch of a Southern Wagon, showing Conestoga influence. See page 118.

to Harper's Ferry, though he did not know what his load was at the time.

The Conestoga wagon gave its name to the Stogie cigar, a great thin coarse one, supposed to have been originally a foot long and made for the delectation of the wagoner.

The prairie schooner and the emigrant wagons of the South had vertical hoops, as had the army wagons of the Civil War.   These

One of the many splendid teams of Swift & Company was sent clear out to the Pacific coast, where it won many prizes at horse shows.
"These noble-looking animals, with round, fat bodies and sleek, glossy coats, are slow in their movements and are not the best for hard and long-continued work; but their proud deportment is well adapted to gratify the ambition of their owner to outvie his neighbor.   As they sweep majestically through the streets of the metropolis, they present a most striking sight to the eye of the stranger."   From "Adaptation of the English Draught Horse for City or Town Work."   Annual Report, 1857, of the U. S. Department of Agriculture.

usually had five bows, supporting a canvas cover.   This was also true of the southern market wagons, which had straight curtains instead of a shaped cover with a draw string, and there was a seat in the front of all of these for the driver.

It is not probable that many Conestogas were made after the Civil War, nor that many were used in that conflict, though previously many crossed the great plains, and the prairie schooner developed from them.   There are pieces of Conestoga hand-forged wagon iron dated as late as 1850 and 1863 in the Landis Valley Museum.

The first Weber wagon was made in Chicago in 1845, and the Studebaker brothers were making their product in South Bend in 1852.   When the national wagon makers came in, the local wagon makers went out, and with them the iron blacksmith, not the horse shoers.   Fifty years ago there were many smith shops struggling along, but today there are few remaining, and not one blacksmith in a dozen can make a good wrought-iron nail.

The wagoner's songs that he sung on the road as he ambled along were doubtless long narrative ones, like the sailor's chanteys. There were Joe Bowers, Camptown Races, Barbara Allen and the Darby Ram — good lusty songs all, with verses that went on and on like the road itself.

View of North Queen Street, Lancaster, about 1840, looking toward the Central Square and showing the railroad which was beginning to replace the Conestoga wagon as a carrier of freight. Courtesy of the Lancaster Trust Company.

The drinking songs of Lancaster County were mostly German, but the tavern songs were English, which was probably true in other parts of Pennsylvania as well. Old Dan Tucker and Captain Jinks of the Horse Marines were great favorites. Other fiddler's tunes were the Arkansas Traveler, Turkey in the Straw, the Fisher's Hornpipe, Pop Goes the Weasel, Money Musk, Yankee Doodle and Wait for the Wagon.

But the Conestoga Wagon was to have a rival. In the Lancaster Intelligencer in July, 1828, is the comment, "We learn that Major

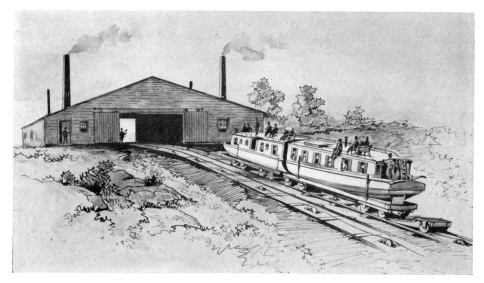

Crossing the Alleghenies in 1840. Sectional canal boat being hauled over the inclined planes of the Portage Railroad.

All Aboard for Pittsburgh — In 1840
    Rear half of sectional canal boat leaving Third and Walnut Streets, Philadelphia (site of the old Stock Exchange Building). These boats, mounted on wheeled trucks, were pulled through the streets by mules or horses, across the old Columbia Avenue Bridge over the Schuylkill River, to what is now Belmont Plateau in Fairmount Park. At this point they were placed upon the Philadelphia and Columbia Railway (which later became the Pennsylvania) and moved by rail to Columbia, Pa. There the sections of the boats were joined and they were placed in the Eastern Division of the Pennsylvania Canal, constructed along the banks of the Susquehanna and Juniata Rivers, and moved to Hollidaysburg, Pa. At this point the boats were removed from the Canal, placed on the Portage Railroad and hauled by eleven inclined planes over the east and west slopes of the Allegheny Mountains to Johnstown, Pa. They were then placed in the Western Division of the Pennsylvania Canal and completed their journey by water to Pittsburgh, the head of navigation on the Ohio River. The journey probably consumed from three days to a week. Charles Dickens, in his "American Notes," has left a memorable account of a ride in one of these boats. From "How the Pennsylvania Railroad has Grown." Courtesy of The Pennsylvania Railroad Co.

The Fairveiw Inn, built 1801.   Three miles from Baltimore.

Wilson has got on as far eastwardly, in locating the Pennsylvania Railroad, as the farm of Colonel Baker in Leacock Township, which is about twenty miles from Columbia." In 1830 this railroad was running, one of the links of an amazing chain of transportation, canals, railroads, inclined planes — but mostly canals — which were known as the "State Works," and which connected Philadelphia and Pittsburgh, and were operated for nearly twenty years without a serious accident.

This was all very well for passenger service — Dickens describes a journey in it in 1842 — but the freighting of the great Conestogas was

not affected until 1852, when the Pennsylvania Railroad opened its through line from Philadelphia to Pittsburgh.

The wagoners voiced their feelings in a song, which seems to have had different verses for every locality, though the plaint was always the same.

"Conestoga Wagons on the National Road," by C. W. Jefferys.
Reproduced from The March of Commerce, Volume IV, The Pageant of America, by permission of the publishers. Copyright, Yale University Press.

Come, all ye bold Wagoners, turn out man by man,
That's opposed to the railroad or any such a plan;
'Tis once I made money by driving my team,
But the goods are now hauled on the railroad by steam.

May the devil get the fellow that invented the plan,
For it'll ruin us poor wagoners and every other man.
It spoils our plantations, wherever it crosses,
And it ruins our markets, we can't sell our hosses.

If we go to Philadelphia, enquiring for a load;
They will tell us directly its gone on the railroad.
The rich folks, this plan they may justly admire,
But it ruins us poor wagoners and it makes our tax higher.

Our states, they are in debt to keep them in repair,
Which causes us poor wagoners to curse and to swear.
It ruins our landlords, it makes business worse,
And upon every other nation it has been a curse.

It ruins wheelright, blacksmiths, and every other trade;
"Damned" all the railroads that ever was made!
It ruins our mechanics, what do you think of it, then?
And it fills our country full of great rich men.

*A Conestoga from the Ford Museum, drawn by an ox team in a pageant celebrating
Dearborn's one hundredth anniversary.*
Courtesy of Mr. J. C. Seacrest, State Journal Co., Lincoln, Nebraska.

The ships, they'll come in with Irishmen by loads,
With their picks and their shovels, to work on the railroads.
When they get on the railroad, its then they are fixed,
They'll fight like the devil with their cudgels and their sticks.

The American with safety, can scarcely ever pass,
For they'll black both his eyes for one word of his "sass."
If it was not for the torment, I'd as leave be in hell,
As upon the railroad, or upon the canal.

Now all ye jolly wagoners who have good wives,
Go home to your farms and there spend your lives;
When your corn is all cribbed and your small grain is sowed,
You'll have nothing to do but curse the railroad.

In 1864, during the Lincoln-McClellan campaign, the Conestoga
wagon, which is now in the Carnegie Museum, appeared in a parade
drawn by thirty-five white horses, one for every state. It was so
imposing that it was used again in 1872.

A model of a Conestoga Wagon and six-horse bell team exhibited by the Pennsylvania Railroad, at the World's Columbian Exposition at Chicago, in 1893.   The original wagon from which this model was copied is thought to have been made about 1834.

Samuel Gingrich, who was born in 1826, was a wagoner of Lancaster County, and freighted between Philadelphia and Pittsburgh. His wagon appeared at the Centennial Exposition in Philadelphia, and was later used by Buffalo Bill, until it was destroyed in a wreck.

Courtesy of
Conestoga National Bank
Lancaster, Pa.

CHAPTER XII

Of some Conestoga Wagons and Wagoners in Franklin County, Pennsylvania

MORE than a hundred years later, Conestoga wagons were still being used on the big Pennsylvania farms, much as George Washington had used his wagon on his Virginia plantations. There were great loads of grain and farm produce to be brought to town, and seed, sugar, salt, and hardware, and many other necessities to be taken back.

From a sketch by Matt A. Daly.

Watering trough hewn from the trunk of a tree and set up so that a horse could get his nose into it without bending his neck very much. The water was pumped into it from the deep well pump made of wooden stocks, extending down below the water line in the well. The hole bored through the center of these stocks was about three inches in diameter and there were rods linked together with a wooden bucket on the end and a leather cap on the top. It was worked by a long pump handle. The cap on the top of the bucket would open when the bucket was submerged, and close when it was lifted up. Unless the well was very deep and it was a long distance down to the water level, about a dozen strokes of the pump handle would bring the water up into the trough.

Wesley Koons, of Franklin County, took great pride and delight in his wagon and horses, as did his son George, who came after him. It was always a thrill to the youngsters to see the six-horse bell team and the big wagon with its tremendous load of corn or wheat being driven through the streets of Greencastle to the grain elevator at the end of the town. Wesley Koons had been a teamster for his father, William Koons, who was a freighter. Later Mr. Koons formed a partnership with David Funk and operated one of the heaviest Conestogas on the road, making his last trip to Baltimore in 1856. On his return he brought a song, called "The Death Song of the Wagoner," and sang it at home. One verse went —

> "It was once I made money by the driving of my team,
> But now the goods are hauled on the railroad by steam;
> I hope the devil will get the fellow that invented the plan
> To ruin us poor wagoners and every other man."

The wagon which Wesley Koons and David Funk owned was burned by the Confederates when they invaded the Cumberland Valley. Mr. Koons later secured another Conestoga that the Confederates had set fire to, near Waterloo, on the South Mountain. This wagon was also a very heavy one and only the middle part was destroyed. From this one the wagon which he used after the Civil War was made. Wesley Koons himself drove his team, also Daddy Wells and his son, John Wells, and finally George Koons. Maybe there were other wagoners.

There was William Logue, of Washington Township, Franklin County, who was a teamster for Henry Besore, who conducted a freight business to and from Baltimore. Six days were allowed for the trip and the teamsters were not permitted to travel on Sunday. James Wells was a teamster, and considered one of the best ones, who drove for different freighters from Washington Township. David Funk was a freighter and Jacob Keckler was a teamster. James and Sharp Walker and Daniel and John Keiser were also wagoners from Franklin County.

Daniel Mickley was one of the early wagoners of Franklin County. He was born in 1795, served as a soldier in the War of 1812, and settled on a farm near the Mason and Dixon line in 1828. Besides being a farmer he was a wagoner, with a six-horse bell team and heavy Conestoga. He made many trips to Baltimore, hauling wheat, whisky and flour to the Baltimore market, and bringing back store goods for the Waynesboro merchants. He retired in 1861.

Tine Elliott was a wagoner of Franklin County who had several teams, the finest of which he drove himself.

For many years after long-distance freighting had passed, the big wagons were still constantly used for shorter hauling on the road, besides doing the hauling from the farm to the town, and often moving people in the Spring of the year. Wesley Koons had eight horses in his team, instead of six, in the Spring of the year, when the roads were bad from excessive rains, and too heavy for six horses to pull through. His bells he had owned for sixty-five or seventy years. He had gotten them from his brother-in-law, Powell Haugh, who had bought them from a man named Mentzer.

How long Mentzer had had them, none know, but their clappers were worn flat. George Koons thinks that they are at least a hundred and fifty years old, and there is a tradition that they came from England. There are twenty-one open bells, grouped in five bows. The bows for the lead horses have five, the middle ones four, and the wheel horse three, all graded in size from two and one-half inches in diameter in front, three and one-half in the middle, and four and one-half on the wheel-horse bow. The bows are made of iron, with

A farm wagon of southeastern Pennsylvania, which also carried freight on the National Pike. This wagon belongs to the Orndorff family of Franklin County. Courtesy of Mr. B. W. Phreaner

pointed prongs on each side, that fitted into staples on the hames. The bows are covered with dog skin, tanned with the hair on, and on each is a bunch of red, white and blue ribbon. There are no bells for the driver's horse in this set. It is said that many a wagoner in trouble would turn his team sharply to the side and break off the tongue, so that passing wagoners could not help him and therefore could not claim his bells.

The fame of Franklin County spread afar, because of the Loudon whip that was made especially for wagoners, at Fort Loudon. It was made by one Andrew McCurdy, who kept several men busy for a number of years, supplying the demand for his product, which was the last word in smartness.

In the later years the Conestoga teams were sure to congregate for any important occasion, knowing that it could not be really important without them. When there was an auction, there was sure to be a ball game in the farm yard on one side of the straw stack or the other, and there were little oyster stoves and candy booths to serve the public. But on the arrival of a six-horse team, all these, and even the auctioneer's jokes, were forgotten. And on election day, when people would all be out on the streets to see the bell teams go through, no one could have been happier or prouder than the driver, unless it was the little boy by the dusty roadside who lived the reality of all his hopes and ambitions in the joy of six great dappled grays, the rumbling of a ponderous white-topped wagon, and the music of the Conestoga bells.

A Road Sign in Nebraska Today

A Conestoga Wagon Hooked Rug

WITH the renewed vogue of the hooked rug, we find those pic-
turing the six-horse bell teams down in Pennsylvania, as
characteristic of the Conestoga country, as are the sailing ships of
New England on the rugs made there.

The rug maker usually makes her own design, and so there is
naturally a great variety. When she has her own memories of the
Conestoga days to put into her handiwork, it adds greatly to the
vividness and charm of her bright picture.

Mrs. Samuel Petersheim, a little Mennonite lady of Berks County,
sends her own description of her rug, which is pictured here. She
says that the wagon stands on the Reading road just before it turns
to the right into Morgantown. In the background stands the manor
house and barns, dated 1776, which were built by Colonel Jacob
Morgan. He served in the French and Indian War, and in 1763 was
rewarded by His Majesty with three thousand acres of land. On
this he built his home, and in 1770 Morgantown became a village.
During the Revolution, George Washington is said to have often been
a guest at the Morgan farm, and local tradition says that an under-
ground passage still connects the house and the barn, built so that
the great general might escape, if the British came.

Mrs. Petersheim's rug is forty-eight inches long and thirty inches
wide.

APPENDIX

WAGONING

There were two classes of these men,
   Men of renown, not well agreed;
Militia men drove narrow treads,
Four horses and plain red Dutch beds,
   And always carried grub and feed;
Because they carried feed and grub
They bore the brunt of many a rub.

These were the thrifty farmer's teams
   That wagoned, only now and then;
They made their trips in winter-time;
They trudged along through rime and grime
   And hurried through it, back again;
An annual trip, or two, they made,
And drove a sort of coastwise trade.

They gathered up promiscuous loads
   Of produce in the neighborhood —
Some whiskey, flour and cloverseeds,
To suit a city dealer's needs,
   And always did the best they could
By hauling these to Baltimore —
Back-loaded for some country-store.

The "Reg'lars" boldly ventured out,
   Despising danger, doubt, and fear;
And, like the gallant merchant-ships,
They made their long, continuous trips
   All through the seasons of the year;
No matter whether cold or warm —
Through heat and cold, through calm and storm.

I see them on their winding way,
   As, in the merry olden time
I saw them, with their heavy loads,
Upon the old-time turnpike-roads,
   The rugged mountains climb;
Like full-rigged ships they seemed to glide
Along the deep-blue mountain-side.

The "Regulars" were haughty men,
   Since *five* or *six* they always drove,
With broad-tread wheels and English beds,
They bore their proud and lofty heads,
   And always thought themselves above
The home-spun, plain, Militia-men,
Who wagoned only now and then.

(Who has not seen, who has not felt
   The cursed arrogance of *purse*!
E'en in the wagoners of the past,
Was seen the haughtiness of caste,
   And felt the old, old, social curse,
That measures manhood by success
More than by native nobleness.)

So were all goods transported then —
   By reg'lar or militia team —
And, though a slow and toilsome way,
It was the best known in its day —
   Before the world had got up steam —
As, now, this steam-dependent world
Is round its business-axle whirled.

I hear the music of the wheels,
   Slow moving o'er the frozen snow;
Like distant bugle-notes they sound,
While from the mountain-heights around,
   Or from the dark-green depths below,
Perchance, the music of the bells
The weird, enchanting, echo swells.

I hear the wagoner's hoarse, harsh voice
   Still urging on the lab'ring steeds;
I hear the sharp crack of his whip —
I see the horses pull and slip,
   Still urged to more herculean deeds —
The while their steaming breath congeals
Like hoar-frost on the wintry fields.

O'er mountain-heights and valleys deep,
   Still, slowly on and on they move,
Along their tedious, rugged way —
Some eighty furlongs in a day —
   Their stalwart strength and faith they prove,
And oft' to their extreme delight,
Some old-time tavern looms to sight.

There, custom always called a halt,
  To water, rest and take a drink;
And, not unlikely, while they stopped
A jig was danced, or horses swapped;
  And so, perchance, a broken link
The smith was hurried to renew,
Or tighten up a loosened shoe,

Meantime, the jolly wagoners stood
  And swaggered 'round the old-time bar —
The latticed nook, the landlord's throne,
Where he presided, all alone,
  And smoked his cheap cigar,
And reckoned up the tippler's bill
For whiskey, at a "fip" a gill;

Or other kinds of old-time drinks,
  All full of good and hearty cheer;
As apple-jacks, and peach-brandies,
Or cider-oils, or sangarees,
  Or, O, the foaming poker'd beer;
Or apple-toddies, steaming hot,
Or cherry-bounce — almost forgot.

There was never a rougher set,
  Or class of men upon the earth,
Than wagoners of the reg'lar line —
Nor jollier when in their wine,
  Around a blazing bar-room hearth;
How they did fiddle, dance and sing?
How did the old-time bar-room ring?

There were few idle fiddles when
  Old wag'ners drank their jolly fill
Of beer and cider by the quart,
And wines and gins of every sort.
  And whiskey, measured by the gill,
And cherry-bounce and cider-oil,
And bitters spiced with penny-royal.

Sometimes the question — who should treat,
  Was left to doubtful luck, or chance;
A game of cards at whist, or loo;
Of checkers, chess, or domino;
  And after that the hoe-down dance;
Sometimes the question — who had beat?
Was settled by the landlord's treat.

Around a blazing hearth, at e'en,
Or roaring ten-plate Pinegrove stove,
Those heroes of the turnpike-roads —
Those haulers of the heavy loads,
    Or weary drivers of a drove,
Foregathered, many a winter's night
In freedom, fun and fond delight.

They sat in all the different ways
That men could sit, or ever sat;
They told of all their jolly days,
And spat in all the different ways
    That men could spit, or ever spat;
They talked of horses and their strength,
And spun their yarns at endless length.

Sometimes they raffled for the stakes,
    And sometimes shot therefor at mark;
A many a foolish wager laid,
And many a reckless swap was made —
    Of horses — traded in the dark;
Sometimes disputes ran wild and high,
To bloody nose or blacken'd eye.

All such disputes were ended quick
By an appeal to harden'd fists;
These were the courts of last resort,
That settled pleas of every sort
    That came upon the wagoner's lists;
No other forum, then, was sought,
When *the* decisive fight was fought.

Ten wagoners in a bar-room — well,
    Say, twenty feet by scant sixteen;
A ten-plate stove, that weighed a ton,
Stood in a wooden-box-spittoon —
    Which was, of course, not very clean —
'Mid clouds of cheap tobacco smoke,
Thick, dark and strong enough to choke.

Huge benches and some pond'rous chairs —
    Such as the world no more may see;
An ample pile of hickory logs.
An old tem-cat and several dogs,
    And playful pups — some two or three —
All 'round one stove or bar-room fire!
A scene an artist might admire.

And, superadded to all these
　　Were unwashed feet and shoes and boots,
And boot-jacks, slippers, tallow dips,
And some great-coats and Loudon whips,
　　And heaps of wagoner's oversuits;
While currying-shirts and overalls
Embellished the surrounding walls.

The recollection of their memory hangs
　　And lingers 'round us like the air;
They haunt us in our waking dreams,
And, often, in our sleep, it seems
　　As if again, we saw them, there;
But stern realities arise
While moisture gathers in our eyes.

　　　　　　H. L. Fisher,
　　　　　　　　York, Pennsylvania, 1888.

TABLE OF DISTANCES

A list of towns, stopping places and their distances, on wagon roads from the "Amerikanischer Stadt und Land Calendaer auf das 1799 Jahr Christi":

MILES

Roads toward the West; from Philadelphia to the Schuylkill............ 2

Thence to —

The Black Horse...................	4
The Prince of Wales..............	4
The Deer.......................	1
The Unicorn....................	5
The Blue Ball..................	4
The Admiral Warren............	3
The White Horse...............	3
Downing's (Mills).............	7
The Ship......................	2
Whitacker......................	8
Douglas........................	3
The Hat........................	4
The Duke of Cumberland..........	3
The Red Lion...................	3
The Conestoga..................	4
Lancaster Court House...........	2
The Scots......................	9
The Bayleys....................	5
The Hughes.....................	4
The Samples...................	5
Swatara.......................	3
The Taylor's..................	3
Harris' Ferry.................	8
Hendricks.....................	3
Chalmers......................	11
Carlisle......................	3
Shippensburgh..................	21
B. Chambers...................	11
Fort Loudon...................	13
Fort Littleton................	18
Juniata.......................	19
Bedford.......................	14
Foot of the Alleghenies........	15
Stony Creek...................	15
Laurel Hill...................	12

MILES

Fort Ligonier...................	9
Pittsburgh.....................	54
Total...........................	320

From Philadelphia to Reading:

To Schneiders..................... 10

Thence to —

Trapp.......................	16
Pottsgrove....................	11
White Horse...................	5
Reading......................	14
Total........................	56

To Jenkintown..................... 10

Thence to —

Craigh's......................	11
The Red Coat..................	11
Dreissbacks...................	12
Easton........................	12
Total........................	56

Reading to Lancaster:

To Adamstown..................... 9

Thence to —

Reamstown.....................	5
Cocalico......................	8
Lancaster.....................	9
Total........................	31

Reading to Harrisburg:

To Womelsdorf..................... 14

Thence to —

Lebanon.......................	14
Hummelstown...................	15
Harrisburg....................	9
Total........................	52

136 r°